The UK

Instant Pot Vortex Air Fryer

Cookbook 2023

1001-Day *Easy Recipes to Fry, Grill, and Roast with Your Instant Pot Vortex Air Fryer*

Emma Reid

Contents

SANDWICHES AND BURGERS RECIPES.....................61

APPETIZERS AND SNACKS 71

VEGETARIANS RECIPES 81

VEGETABLE SIDE DISHES RECIPES.....................91

INTRODUCTION

How Does an Air Fryer Work?

The first think you're probably wondering is how an Air Fryer works. How is it any different than a regular deep fryer or an oven? Most importantly, Air Fryers are different from regular deep fryers because they don't actually fry food, meaning you don't actually submerge your food in hot oil to cook it.

The actual mechanism of Air Fryers is most akin to that of a convection oven. Basically, your food is placed in a perforated metal basket. At the top is a heating unit with a high powered fan that blows the hot air all around the food, creating a convection effect that nicely and evenly browns the outside of the food. And unlike a convection oven, Air Fryers are compact, allowing for faster and more efficient preheating and cooking times.

10 Reasons to Buy an Air Fryer

1) It makes delicious food !

When you bake food in regular ovens (especially not convention ovens), you are often left with uneven results, with some parts burnt and other parts undercooked. The mechanism of Air Fryers described above allows hot air to circulate all around the food, maximizing surface area-to-heat ratio and allowing for perfectly even crispiness and crunchiness. While an Air Fryer won't taste exactly like if you used a traditional deep fryer, we really love the end result of each recipe we've tried so far.

2) It is a healthier option

Love the taste of fried food but not the way it makes you feel afterwards (for instance Zoe tends to get heartburn with fried food)? Are you disappointed with the end result when you try the oven-roasted version of the same recipe? If yes to these questions, then an Air Fryer might be the solution!

You can usually get away with using little-to-no oil when cooking with an Air Fryer, which can cut calories. Furthermore, one study (Sansano et at., 2015) showed that compared to traditional frying methods, using an air fryer reduces acrylamide (a compound associated with certain types of cancer) by up to 90%.

3) It is time and energy efficient

With their compact size and efficient circulation of hot air, Air Fryers out-compete your oven. With most recipes only needing 8-20 minutes of cooking, Air Fryers reduce cooking time by up to 25% (they also only need a fraction of the time to preheat, unlike your oven), saving you both time and energy.

4) There's an air fryer for every price range

With prices as low as $40, buying an Air Fryer doesn't have to break your wallet. We are obviously more than happy with our investment in an Air Fryer. And don't worry, even the lower-priced ones still produce great results! Keep reading this Ultimate Air Fryer Guide to see the specific products we recommend.

5) They are easy to clean

With removable parts, nonstick materials, and most being dishwasher-safe, cleaning your air fryer is no hassle at all! And compared to the grease that coats your kitchen walls after deep frying foods, an Air Fryer produces no mess.

6) They are versatile and can make all kinds of recipes

See below for a sample of all of the different types of food you can make using an Air Fryer. From meat to vegetables to even pizza, we've been able to incorporate air frying into a ton of our meal preparations.

7) Many have different modes, allowing different types of cooking

Not only used for frying foods, an Air Fryer can also be used for reheating leftovers, thawing frozen food, and much, much more. Ours lets you change the settings to "air fry", "roast", "dehydrate", and "reheat". It's up to you to experiment!

8) They come in all different shapes and sizes

It's true that they take up some counter space. But there's an Air Fryer of every size to fit your needs. If you mostly cook for one or two people, you can get away with 2 to 3 quart sized Air Fryers. If you usually cook for a family of 3-5, consider 5 to 6 quart ones. But generally, air fryers between 3 to 5 quarts are versatile enough for most types and quantities of cooking.

9) They make for a great gift

What a perfect gift for the budding home chef?! I got ours for Zoe for Christmas. But whether its for a birthday, wedding registry, or any other special occasion, an Air Fryer makes for an ideal long-lasting and useful present.

10) They let you join the Air Fryer community

With niche Air Fryer blogs to Air Fryer recipe books, buying one of these lets you drastically expand your culinary repertoire and connect with a whole new community of home chefs.

HOW TO USE AN AIR FRYER

The Air Fryer's Versatility

Get ready to challenge everything you know about frying foods. Air fryers can fry your favorite foods to crispy, golden brown perfection (yes, French fries and potato chips!) using little or no oil. Not only can you make traditionally fried foods like potato chips and French fries, but it's also great for vegetables, proteins like chicken wings and drummettes, and appetizers like coquettes and feta triangles. Even desserts like brownies and blondies are perfectly baked in an air fryer.

Why It Works

Put in other terms, an air fryer is much like a convection oven but in a different outfit, cooking food at very high temperatures while simultaneously circulating dry air around the food, cooking food faster all the while making it crisp without needing to add extra fat.

What to Look for in an Air Fryer

There are a lot of different sizes and types of air fryers available now. If you're cooking for a crowd, try an the Philips XXL Air Fryer which can cook an entire chicken or six portions of fries.

If you have limited counter space, try the Philips Avance Air Fryer which uses patented technology to circulate hot air, yielding crunchy, satisfying results. and this next-generation air fryer boasts a more compact size (same capacity!) and TurboStar technology, which ensures food cooks evenly (no more worrying about pile-ups). Now you can enjoy all the fried foods you love—without the guilt.

To up an air fryer's versatility even more, You can also buy a variety of different attachments, such as a rack, grill pan, muffin pans and mesh baskets) to for entertaining. Check out our Air Fryer seasonings that we developed in-house, ranging from Buttermilk Black Pepper Seasoning for air-frying chicken to Garlic Sichuan Seasoning perfect for Chinese cooking.

Read on for a video on the air fryer in action, how-to tips and our favorite recipes, including those fries, air-fried tonkotsu, chicken wings and more.

Five Tips for Using an Air Fryer

1. Shake it.

Be sure to open the air fryer and shake foods around as they "fry" in the machine's basket—smaller foods like French fries and chips can compress. For best results, rotate them every 5-10 minutes.

2. Don't overcrowd.

Give foods plenty of space so that the air can circulate effectively; that's what gives you crispy results. Our test kitchen cooks swear by the air fryer for snacks and small batches.

3. Give foods a spray.

Lightly spray foods with cooking spray or add just a bit of oil to ensure they don't stick to the basket.

4. Keep it dry.

Pat foods dry before cooking (if they are marinated, for example) to avoid splattering and excess smoke. Similarly, when cooking high-fat foods like chicken wings, make sure to empty the fat from the bottom machine periodically.

5. Master other cooking methods.

The air fryer isn't just for frying; it's great for other healthy cooking methods like baking, roasting and grilling, too. Our test kitchen also loves to use the machine for cooking salmon!

BREAD AND BREAKFAST

Broccoli Cornbread

🥣 Servings: 6	🍲 Cooking Time: 18 Mins.

Ingredients:

- 1 C. frozen chopped broccoli, thawed and drained
- ¼ C. cottage cheese
- 1 egg, beaten
- 2 tbsp. minced onion
- 2 tbsp. melted butter
- ½ C. flour
- ½ C. yellow cornmeal
- 1 tsp. baking powder
- ½ tsp. salt
- ¼ C. milk, plus 2 tablespoons
- cooking spray

Directions:

1. Place thawed broccoli in colander and press with a spoon to squeeze out excess moisture.
2. Stir together all ingredients in a large bowl.
3. Spray 6 x 6-inch baking pan with cooking spray.
4. Spread batter in pan and cook at 330°F for 18 Mins. or until cornbread is lightly browned and loaf starts to pull away from sides of pan.

Tuscan Toast

Ingredients:

♦ ¼ C. butter

♦ ½ tsp. lemon juice

♦ ½ clove garlic

♦ ½ tsp. dried parsley flakes

♦ 4 slices Italian bread, 1-inch thick

Directions:

1. Place butter, lemon juice, garlic, and parsley in a food processor. Process about 1 minute, or until garlic is pulverized and ingredients are well blended.

2. Spread garlic butter on both sides of bread slices.

3. Place bread slices upright in air fryer basket. (They can lie flat but cook better standing on end.)

4. Cook at 390°F for 5minutes or until toasty brown.

Cheddar Cheese Biscuits

🥣 Servings: 8	🍲 Cooking Time: 22 Mins.

Ingredients:

- 2⅓ C. self-rising flour
- 2 tbsp. sugar
- ½ C. butter (1 stick), frozen for 15 Mins.
- ½ C. grated Cheddar cheese, plus more to melt on top
- 1⅓ C. buttermilk
- 1 C. all-purpose flour, for shaping
- 1 tbsp. butter, melted

Directions:

1. Line a buttered 7-inch metal cake pan with parchment paper or a silicone liner.

2. Combine the flour and sugar in a large mixing bowl. Grate the butter into the flour. Add the grated cheese and stir to coat the cheese and butter with flour. Then add the buttermilk and stir just until you can no longer see streaks of flour. The dough should be quite wet.

3. Spread the all-purpose (not self-rising) flour out on a small cookie sheet. With a spoon, scoop 8 evenly sized balls of dough into the flour, making sure they don't touch each other. With floured hands, coat each dough ball with flour and toss them gently from hand to hand to shake off any excess flour. Place each floured dough ball into the prepared pan, right up next to the other. This will help the biscuits rise up, rather than spreading out.

4. Preheat the air fryer to 380°F.

5. Transfer the cake pan to the basket of the air fryer, lowering it into the basket using a sling made of aluminum foil (fold a piece of aluminum foil into a strip about 2-inches wide by 24-inches long). Let the ends of the aluminum foil sling hang across the cake pan before returning the basket to the air fryer.

6. Air-fry for 20 minutes. Check the biscuits a couple of times to make sure they are not getting too brown on top. If they are, re-arrange the aluminum foil strips to cover any brown parts. After 20 minutes, check the biscuits by inserting a toothpick into the center of the biscuits. It should come out clean. If it needs a little more time, continue to air-fry for a couple of extra minutes. Brush the tops of the biscuits with some melted butter and sprinkle a little more grated cheese on top if desired. Pop the basket back into the air fryer for another 2 minutes. Remove the cake pan from the air fryer using the aluminum sling. Let the biscuits cool for just a minute or two and then turn them out onto a plate and pull apart. Serve immediately.

Garlic-cheese Biscuits

Ingredients:

- 1 C. self-rising flour
- 1 tsp. garlic powder
- 2 tbsp. butter, diced
- 2 oz. sharp Cheddar cheese, grated
- ½ C. milk
- cooking spray

Directions:

1. Preheat air fryer to 330°F.
2. Combine flour and garlic in a medium bowl and stir together.
3. Using a pastry blender or knives, cut butter into dry ingredients.
4. Stir in cheese.
5. Add milk and stir until stiff dough forms.
6. If dough is too sticky to handle, stir in 1 or 2 more tbsp. of self-rising flour before shaping. Biscuits should be firm enough to hold their shape. Otherwise, they'll stick to the air fryer basket.
7. Divide dough into 8 portions and shape into 2-inch biscuits about ¾-inch thick.
8. Spray air fryer basket with nonstick cooking spray.
9. Place all 8 biscuits in basket and cook at 330°F for 8 minutes.

Fry Bread

Ingredients:

- 1 C. flour
- 2 tsp. baking powder
- ¼ tsp. salt
- ¼ C. lukewarm milk
- 1 tsp. oil
- 2–3 tbsp. water
- oil for misting or cooking spray

Directions:

1. Stir together flour, baking powder, and salt. Gently mix in the milk and oil. Stir in 1 tbsp. water. If needed, add more water 1 tbsp. at a time until stiff dough forms. Dough shouldn't be sticky, so use only as much as you need.

2. Divide dough into 4 portions and shape into balls. Cover with a towel and let rest for 10minutes.

3. Preheat air fryer to 390°F.

4. Shape dough as desired:

5. a. Pat into 3-inch circles. This will make a thicker bread to eat plain or with a sprinkle of cinnamon or honey butter. You can cook all 4 at once.

6. b. Pat thinner into rectangles about 3 x 6 inches. This will create a thinner bread to serve as a base for dishes such as Indian tacos. The circular shape is more traditional, but rectangles allow you to cook 2 at a time in your air fryer basket.

7. Spray both sides of dough pieces with oil or cooking spray.

8. Place the 4 circles or 2 of the dough rectangles in the air fryer basket and cook at 390°F for 3minutes. Spray tops, turn, spray other side, and cook for 2 more minutes. If necessary, repeat to cook remaining bread.

9. Serve piping hot as is or allow to cool slightly and add toppings to create your own Native American tacos.

Breakfast Pot Pies

Servings: 4　　　**Cooking Time: 20 Mins.**

Ingredients:

- 1 refrigerated pie crust
- ½ lb. pork breakfast sausage
- ¼ C. diced onion
- 1 garlic clove, minced
- ½ tsp. ground black pepper
- ¼ tsp. salt
- 1 C. chopped bell peppers
- 1 C. roasted potatoes
- 2 C. milk
- 2 to 3 tbsp. all-purpose flour

Directions:

1. Flatten the store-bought pie crust out on an even surface. Cut 4 equal circles that are slightly larger than the circumference of ramekins (by about ¼ inch). Set aside.

2. In a medium pot, sauté the breakfast sausage with the onion, garlic, black pepper, and salt. When browned, add in the bell peppers and potatoes and cook an additional 3 to 4 Mins. to soften the bell peppers. Remove from the heat and portion equally into the ramekins.

3. To the same pot (without washing it), add the milk. Heat over medium-high heat until boiling. Slowly reduce to a simmer and stir in the flour, 1 tbsp. at a time, until the gravy thickens and coats the back of a wooden spoon (about 5 minutes).

4. Remove from the heat and equally portion ½ C. of gravy into each ramekin on top of the sausage and potato mixture.

5. Place the circle pie crusts on top of the ramekins, lightly pressing them down on the perimeter of each ramekin with the prongs of a fork. Gently poke the prongs into the center top of the pie crust a few times to create holes for the steam to escape as the pie cooks.

6. Bake in the air fryer for 6 Mins. (or until the tops are golden brown).

7. Remove and let cool 5 Mins. before serving.

Western Frittata

Servings: 1   **Cooking Time: 19 Mins.**

Ingredients:

- ½ red or green bell pepper, cut into ½-inch chunks
- 1 tsp. olive oil
- 3 eggs, beaten
- ¼ C. grated Cheddar cheese
- ¼ C. diced cooked ham
- salt and freshly ground black pepper, to taste
- 1 tsp. butter
- 1 tsp. chopped fresh parsley

Directions:

1. Preheat the air fryer to 400°F.
2. Toss the peppers with the olive oil and air-fry for 6 minutes, shaking the basket once or twice during the cooking process to redistribute the ingredients.
3. While the vegetables are cooking, beat the eggs well in a bowl, stir in the Cheddar cheese and ham, and season with salt and freshly ground black pepper. Add the air-fried peppers to this bowl when they have finished cooking.
4. Place a 6- or 7-inch non-stick metal cake pan into the air fryer basket with the butter using an aluminum sling to lower the pan into the basket. (Fold a piece of aluminum foil into a strip about 2-inches wide by 24-inches long.) Air-fry for 1 minute at 380°F to melt the butter. Remove the cake pan and rotate the pan to distribute the butter and grease the pan. Pour the egg mixture into the cake pan and return the pan to the air fryer, using the aluminum sling.
5. Air-fry at 380°F for 12 minutes, or until the frittata has puffed up and is lightly browned. Let the frittata sit in the air fryer for 5 Mins. to cool to an edible temperature and set up. Remove the cake pan from the air fryer, sprinkle with parsley and serve immediately.

Strawberry Streusel Muffins

Servings: 12　　**Cooking Time: 14 Mins.**

Ingredients:

- 1¾ C. all-purpose flour
- ½ C. granulated sugar
- 2 tsp. baking powder
- ¼ tsp. baking soda
- ½ tsp. salt
- ½ C. plain yogurt
- ½ C. milk
- ¼ C. vegetable oil
- 2 large eggs
- 1 tsp. vanilla extract
- ½ C. freeze-dried strawberries
- 2 tbsp. brown sugar
- ¼ C. oats
- 2 tbsp. butter

Directions:

1. Preheat the air fryer to 330°F.
2. In a large bowl, whisk together the flour, sugar, baking powder, baking soda, and salt; set aside.
3. In a separate bowl, whisk together the yogurt, milk, vegetable oil, eggs, and vanilla extract.
4. Make a well in the dry ingredients; then pour the wet ingredients into the well of the dry ingredients. Using a rubber spatula, mix the ingredients for 1 minute or until slightly lumpy. Fold in the strawberries.
5. In a small bowl, use your fingers to mix together the brown sugar, oats, and butter until coarse crumbles appear. Divide the mixture in half.
6. Using silicone muffin liners, fill 6 muffin liners two-thirds full.
7. Crumble half of the streusel topping onto the first batch of muffins.
8. Carefully place the muffin liners in the air fryer basket and bake for 14 Mins. (or until the tops are browned and a toothpick inserted in the center comes out clean). Carefully remove the muffins from the basket and repeat with the remaining batter and topping.
9. Serve warm.

Seasoned Herbed Sourdough Croutons

Servings: 4 **Cooking Time: 7 Mins.**

Ingredients:

- 4 C. cubed sourdough bread, 1-inch cubes (about 8 ounces)
- 1 tbsp. olive oil
- 1 tsp. fresh thyme leaves
- ¼ – ½ tsp. salt
- freshly ground black pepper

Directions:

1. Combine all ingredients in a bowl and taste to make sure it is seasoned to your liking.
2. Preheat the air fryer to 400°F.
3. Toss the bread cubes into the air fryer and air-fry for 7 minutes, shaking the basket once or twice while they cook.
4. Serve warm or store in an airtight container.

DESSERTS AND SWEETS

Fried Banana S'mores

Ingredients:

- ◆ 4 bananas
- ◆ 3 tbsp. mini semi-sweet chocolate chips
- ◆ 3 tbsp. mini peanut butter chips
- ◆ 3 tbsp. mini marshmallows
- ◆ 3 tbsp. graham cracker cereal

Directions:

1. Preheat the air fryer to 400°F.
2. Slice into the un-peeled bananas lengthwise along the inside of the curve, but do not slice through the bottom of the peel. Open the banana slightly to form a pocket.
3. Fill each pocket with chocolate chips, peanut butter chips and marshmallows. Poke the graham cracker cereal into the filling.
4. Place the bananas in the air fryer basket, resting them on the side of the basket and each other to keep them upright with the filling facing up. Air-fry for 6 minutes, or until the bananas are soft to the touch, the peels have blackened and the chocolate and marshmallows have melted and toasted.
5. Let them cool for a couple of Mins. and then simply serve with a spoon to scoop out the filling.

Thumbprint Sugar Cookies

Servings: 10   **Cooking Time: 8 Mins.**

Ingredients:

- 2½ tbsp. butter
- ⅓ C. cane sugar
- 1 tsp. pure vanilla extract
- 1 large egg
- 1 C. all-purpose flour
- ½ tsp. baking soda
- ¼ tsp. salt
- 10 chocolate kisses

Directions:

1. Preheat the air fryer to 350°F.
2. In a large bowl, cream the butter with the sugar and vanilla. Whisk in the egg and set aside.
3. In a separate bowl, mix the flour, baking soda, and salt. Then gently mix the dry ingredients into the wet. Portion the dough into 10 balls; then press down on each with the bottom of a C. to create a flat cookie.
4. Liberally spray the metal trivet of an air fryer basket with olive oil mist.
5. Place the cookies in the air fryer basket on the trivet and cook for 8 Mins. or until the tops begin to lightly brown.
6. Remove and immediately press the chocolate kisses into the tops of the cookies while still warm.
7. Let cool 5 Mins. and then enjoy.

Mixed Berry Hand Pies

 Servings: 4   **Cooking Time: 15 Mins.**

Ingredients:

- ¾ C. sugar
- ½ tsp. ground cinnamon
- 1 tbsp. cornstarch
- 1 C. blueberries
- 1 C. blackberries
- 1 C. raspberries, divided
- 1 tsp. water
- 1 package refrigerated pie dough (or your own homemade pie dough)
- 1 egg, beaten

Directions:

1. Combine the sugar, cinnamon, and cornstarch in a small saucepan. Add the blueberries, blackberries, and ½ C. of the raspberries. Toss the berries gently to coat them evenly. Add the tsp. of water to the saucepan and turn the stovetop on to medium-high heat, stirring occasionally. Once the berries break down, release their juice and start to simmer (about 5 minutes), simmer for another couple of Mins. and then transfer the mixture to a bowl, stir in the remaining ½ C. of raspberries and let it cool.

2. Preheat the air fryer to 370°F.

3. Cut the pie dough into four 5-inch circles and four 6-inch circles.

4. Spread the 6-inch circles on a flat surface. Divide the berry filling between all four circles. Brush the perimeter of the dough circles with a little water. Place the 5-inch circles on top of the filling and press the perimeter of the dough circles together to seal. Roll the edges of the bottom circle up over the top circle to make a crust around the filling. Press a fork around the crust to make decorative indentations and to seal the crust shut. Brush the pies with egg wash and sprinkle a little sugar on top. Poke a small hole in the center of each pie with a paring knife to vent the dough.

5. Air-fry two pies at a time. Brush or spray the air fryer basket with oil and place the pies into the basket. Air-fry for 9 minutes. Turn the pies over and air-fry for another 6 minutes. Serve warm or at room temperature.

Giant Buttery Chocolate Chip Cookie

Ingredients:

- ⅔ C. plus 1 tbsp. All-purpose flour
- ¼ tsp. Baking soda
- ¼ tsp. Table salt
- Baking spray (see the headnote)
- 4 tbsp. (¼ cup/½ stick) plus 1 tsp. Butter, at room temperature
- ¼ C. plus 1 tsp. Packed dark brown sugar
- 3 tbsp. plus 1 tsp. Granulated white sugar
- 2½ tbsp. Pasteurized egg substitute, such as Egg Beaters
- ½ tsp. Vanilla extract
- ¾ C. plus 1 tbsp. Semisweet or bittersweet chocolate chips

Directions:

1. Preheat the air fryer to 350°F .
2. Whisk the flour, baking soda, and salt in a bowl until well combined.
3. For a small air fryer, coat the inside of a 6-inch round cake pan with baking spray. For a medium air fryer, coat the inside of a 7-inch round cake pan with baking spray. And for a large air fryer, coat the inside of an 8-inch round cake pan with baking spray.
4. Using a hand electric mixer at medium speed, beat the butter, brown sugar, and granulated white sugar in a bowl until smooth and thick, about 3 minutes, scraping down the inside of the bowl several times.
5. Beat in the pasteurized egg substitute or egg (as applicable) and vanilla until uniform. Scrape down and remove the beaters. Fold in the flour mixture and chocolate chips with a rubber spatula, just until combined. Scrape and gently press this dough into the prepared pan, getting it even across the pan to the perimeter.
6. Set the pan in the basket and air-fry undisturbed for 16 minutes, or until the cookie is puffed, browned, and feels set to the touch.
7. Transfer the pan to a wire rack and cool for 10 minutes. Loosen the cookie from the perimeter with a spatula, then invert the pan onto a cutting board and let the cookie come free. Remove the pan and reinvert the cookie onto the wire rack. Cool for 5 Mins. more before slicing into wedges to serve.

Fried Twinkies

Ingredients:

- 2 Large egg white(s)
- 2 tbsp. Water
- 1½ C. (about 9 ounces) Ground gingersnap cookie crumbs
- 6 Twinkies
- Vegetable oil spray

Directions:

1. Preheat the air fryer to 400°F.
2. Set up and fill two shallow soup plates or small pie plates on your counter: one for the egg white(s), whisked with the water until foamy; and one for the gingersnap crumbs.
3. Dip a Twinkie in the egg white(s), turning it to coat on all sides, even the ends. Let the excess egg white mixture slip back into the rest, then set the Twinkie in the crumbs. Roll it to coat on all sides, even the ends, pressing gently to get an even coating. Then repeat this process: egg white(s), followed by crumbs. Lightly coat the prepared Twinkie on all sides with vegetable oil spray. Set aside and coat each of the remaining Twinkies with the same double-dipping technique, followed by spraying.
4. Set the Twinkies flat side up in the basket with as much air space between them as possible. Air-fry for 5 minutes, or until browned and crunchy.
5. Use a nonstick-safe spatula to gently transfer the Twinkies to a wire rack. Cool for at least 10 Mins. before serving.

Coconut Crusted Bananas With Pineapple Sauce

Ingredients:

- Pineapple Sauce
- 1½ C. puréed fresh pineapple
- 2 tbsp. sugar
- juice of 1 lemon
- ¼ tsp. ground cinnamon
- 3 firm bananas
- ¼ C. sweetened condensed milk
- 1¼ C. shredded coconut
- ⅓ C. crushed graham crackers (crumbs)
- vegetable or canola oil, in a spray bottle
- vanilla frozen yogurt or ice cream

Directions:

1. Make the pineapple sauce by combining the pineapple, sugar, lemon juice and cinnamon in a saucepan. Simmer the mixture on the stovetop for 20 minutes, and then set it aside.

2. Slice the bananas diagonally into ½-inch thick slices and place them in a bowl. Pour the sweetened condensed milk into the bowl and toss the bananas gently to coat. Combine the coconut and graham cracker crumbs together in a shallow dish. Remove the banana slices from the condensed milk and let any excess milk drip off. Dip the banana slices in the coconut and crumb mixture to coat both sides. Spray the coated slices with oil.

3. Preheat the air fryer to 400°F.

4. Grease the bottom of the air fryer basket with a little oil. Air-fry the bananas in batches at 400°F for 5 minutes, turning them over halfway through the cooking time. Air-fry until the bananas are golden brown on both sides.

5. Serve warm over vanilla frozen yogurt with some of the pineapple sauce spooned over top.

Chewy Coconut Cake

Servings: 6 **Cooking Time: 18-22 Mins.**

Ingredients:

- ¾ C. plus 2½ tbsp. All-purpose flour
- ¾ tsp. Baking powder
- ⅛ tsp. Table salt
- 7½ tbsp. (1 stick minus ½ tablespoon) Butter, at room temperature
- ⅓ C. plus 1 tbsp. Granulated white sugar
- 5 tbsp. Packed light brown sugar
- 5 tbsp. Pasteurized egg substitute, such as Egg Beaters
- 2 tsp. Vanilla extract
- ½ C. Unsweetened shredded coconut (see here)
- Baking spray

Directions:

1. Preheat the air fryer to 325°F (or 330°F, if that's the closest setting).
2. Mix the flour, baking powder, and salt in a small bowl until well combined.
3. Using an electric hand mixer at medium speed , beat the butter, granulated white sugar, and brown sugar in a medium bowl until creamy and smooth, about 3 minutes, occasionally scraping down the inside of the bowl. Beat in the egg substitute or egg and vanilla until smooth.
4. Scrape down and remove the beaters. Fold in the flour mixture with a rubber spatula just until all the flour is moistened. Fold in the coconut until the mixture is a uniform color.
5. Use the baking spray to generously coat the inside of a 6-inch round cake pan for a small batch, a 7-inch round cake pan for a medium batch, or an 8-inch round cake pan for a large batch. Scrape and spread the batter into the pan, smoothing the batter out to an even layer.
6. Set the pan in the basket and air-fry for 18 Mins. for a 6-inch layer, 20 Mins. for a 7-inch layer, or 22 Mins. for an 8-inch layer, or until the cake is well browned and set even if there's a little soft give right at the center. Start checking it at the 16-minute mark to know where you are.
7. Use hot pads or silicone baking mitts to transfer the cake pan to a wire rack. Cool for at least 1 hour or up to 4 hours. Use a nonstick-safe knife to slice the cake into wedges right in the pan, lifting them out one by one.

Strawberry Pastry Rolls

Ingredients:

- 3 oz. low-fat cream cheese
- 2 tbsp. plain yogurt
- 2 tsp. sugar
- ¼ tsp. pure vanilla extract
- 8 oz. fresh strawberries
- 8 sheets phyllo dough
- butter-flavored cooking spray
- ¼–½ C. dark chocolate chips (optional)

Directions:

1. In a medium bowl, combine the cream cheese, yogurt, sugar, and vanilla. Beat with hand mixer at high speed until smooth, about 1 minute.
2. Wash strawberries and destem. Chop enough of them to measure ½ cup. Stir into cheese mixture.
3. Preheat air fryer to 330°F.
4. Phyllo dough dries out quickly, so cover your stack of phyllo sheets with waxed paper and then place a damp dish towel on top of that. Remove only one sheet at a time as you work.
5. To create one pastry roll, lay out a single sheet of phyllo. Spray lightly with butter-flavored spray, top with a second sheet of phyllo, and spray the second sheet lightly.
6. Place a quarter of the filling (about 3 tablespoons) about ½ inch from the edge of one short side. Fold the end of the phyllo over the filling and keep rolling a turn or two. Fold in both the left and right sides so that the edges meet in the middle of your roll. Then roll up completely. Spray outside of pastry roll with butter spray.
7. When you have 4 rolls, place them in the air fryer basket, seam side down, leaving some space in between each. Cook at 330°F for 6 minutes, until they turn a delicate golden brown.
8. Repeat step 7 for remaining rolls.
9. Allow pastries to cool to room temperature.
10. When ready to serve, slice the remaining strawberries. If desired, melt the chocolate chips in microwave or double boiler. Place 1 pastry on each dessert plate, and top with sliced strawberries. Drizzle melted chocolate over strawberries and onto plate.

Puff Pastry Apples

 Servings: 4   **Cooking Time: 10 Mins.**

Ingredients:

- 3 Rome or Gala apples, peeled
- 2 tbsp. sugar
- 1 tsp. all-purpose flour
- 1 tsp. ground cinnamon
- ⅛ tsp. ground ginger
- pinch ground nutmeg
- 1 sheet puff pastry

- 1 tbsp. butter, cut into 4 pieces
- 1 egg, beaten
- vegetable oil
- vanilla ice cream (optional)
- caramel sauce (optional)

Directions:

1. Remove the core from the apple by cutting the four sides off the apple around the core. Slice the pieces of apple into thin half-moons, about ¼-inch thick. Combine the sugar, flour, cinnamon, ginger, and nutmeg in a large bowl. Add the apples to the bowl and gently toss until the apples are evenly coated with the spice mixture. Set aside.

2. Cut the puff pastry sheet into a 12-inch by 12-inch square. Then quarter the sheet into four 6-inch squares. Save any remaining pastry for decorating the apples at the end.

3. Divide the spiced apples between the four puff pastry squares, stacking the apples in the center of each square and placing them flat on top of each other in a circle. Top the apples with a piece of the butter.

4. Brush the four edges of the pastry with the egg wash. Bring the four corners of the pastry together, wrapping them around the apple slices and pinching them together at the top in the style of a "beggars purse" appetizer. Fold the ends of the pastry corners down onto the apple making them look like leaves. Brush the entire apple with the egg wash.

5. Using the leftover dough, make leaves to decorate the apples. Cut out 8 leaf shapes, about 1½-inches long, "drawing" the leaf veins on the pastry leaves with a paring knife. Place 2 leaves on the top of each apple, tucking the ends of the leaves under the pastry in the center of the apples. Brush the top of the leaves with additional egg wash. Sprinkle the entire apple with some granulated sugar.

6. Preheat the air fryer to 350°F.

7. Spray or brush the inside of the air fryer basket with oil. Place the apples in the basket and air-fry for 6 minutes. Carefully turn the apples over – it's easiest to remove one apple, then flip the others over and finally return the last apple to the air fryer. Air-fry for an additional 4 minutes.

8. Serve the puff pastry apples warm with vanilla ice cream and drizzle with some caramel sauce.

BEEF, PORK & LAMB RECIPES

Smokehouse-style Beef Ribs

🍲 Servings: 3　　🍲 Cooking Time: 25 Mins.

Ingredients:

- ¼ tsp. Mild smoked paprika
- ¼ tsp. Garlic powder
- ¼ tsp. Onion powder
- ¼ tsp. Table salt
- ¼ tsp. Ground black pepper
- 3 10- to 12-ounce beef back ribs (not beef short ribs)

Directions:

1. Preheat the air fryer to 350°F .
2. Mix the smoked paprika, garlic powder, onion powder, salt, and pepper in a small bowl until uniform. Massage and pat this mixture onto the ribs.
3. When the machine is at temperature, set the ribs in the basket in one layer, turning them on their sides if necessary, sort of like they're spooning but with at least ¼ inch air space between them. Air-fry for 25 minutes, turning once, until deep brown and sizzling.
4. Use kitchen tongs to transfer the ribs to a wire rack. Cool for 5 Mins. before serving.

Boneless Ribeyes

Ingredients:

- 2 8-ounce boneless ribeye steaks
- 4 tsp. Worcestershire sauce
- ½ tsp. garlic powder
- pepper
- 4 tsp. extra virgin olive oil
- salt

Directions:

1. Season steaks on both sides with Worcestershire sauce. Use the back of a spoon to spread evenly.
2. Sprinkle both sides of steaks with garlic powder and coarsely ground black pepper to taste.
3. Drizzle both sides of steaks with olive oil, again using the back of a spoon to spread evenly over surfaces.
4. Allow steaks to marinate for 30minutes.
5. Place both steaks in air fryer basket and cook at 390°F for 5minutes.
6. Turn steaks over and cook until done:
    1. Medium rare: additional 5 Mins.
    2. Medium: additional 7 Mins.
    3. Well done: additional 10 Mins.
7. Remove steaks from air fryer basket and let sit 5minutes. Salt to taste and serve.

Meat Loaves

Ingredients:

- Sauce
- ¼ C. white vinegar
- ¼ C. brown sugar
- 2 tbsp. Worcestershire sauce
- ½ C. ketchup
- Meat Loaves
- 1 lb. very lean ground beef
- ⅔ C. dry bread (approx. 1 slice torn into small pieces)
- 1 egg
- ⅓ C. minced onion
- 1 tsp. salt
- 2 tbsp. ketchup

Directions:

1. In a small saucepan, combine all sauce ingredients and bring to a boil. Remove from heat and stir to ensure that brown sugar dissolves completely.
2. In a large bowl, combine the beef, bread, egg, onion, salt, and ketchup. Mix well.
3. Divide meat mixture into 4 portions and shape each into a thick, round patty. Patties will be about 3 to 3½ inches in diameter, and all four should fit easily into the air fryer basket at once.
4. Cook at 360°F for 18 minutes, until meat is well done. Baste tops of mini loaves with a small amount of sauce, and cook 1 minute.
5. Serve hot with additional sauce on the side.

Pretzel-coated Pork Tenderloin

Ingredients:

- 1 Large egg white(s)
- 2 tsp. Dijon mustard (gluten-free, if a concern)
- 1½ C. (about 6 ounces) Crushed pretzel crumbs (see the headnote; gluten-free, if a concern)
- 1 lb. (4 sections) Pork tenderloin, cut into ¼-pound (4-ounce) sections
- Vegetable oil spray

Directions:

1. Preheat the air fryer to 350°F .

2. Set up and fill two shallow soup plates or small pie plates on your counter: one for the egg white(s), whisked with the mustard until foamy; and one for the pretzel crumbs.

3. Dip a section of pork tenderloin in the egg white mixture and turn it to coat well, even on the ends. Let any excess egg white mixture slip back into the rest, then set the pork in the pretzel crumbs. Roll it several times, pressing gently, until the pork is evenly coated, even on the ends. Generously coat the pork section with vegetable oil spray, set it aside, and continue coating and spraying the remaining sections.

4. Set the pork sections in the basket with at least ¼ inch between them. Air-fry undisturbed for 10 minutes, or until an instant-read meat thermometer inserted into the center of one section registers 145°F.

5. Use kitchen tongs to transfer the pieces to a wire rack. Cool for 3 to 5 Mins. before serving.

Calf's Liver

 Servings: 4   **Cooking Time: 5 Mins.**

Ingredients:

- ♦ 1 lb. sliced calf's liver
- ♦ salt and pepper
- ♦ 2 eggs
- ♦ 2 tbsp. milk
- ♦ ½ C. whole wheat flour
- ♦ 1½ C. panko breadcrumbs
- ♦ ½ C. plain breadcrumbs
- ♦ ½ tsp. salt
- ♦ ¼ tsp. pepper
- ♦ oil for misting or cooking spray

Directions:

1. Cut liver slices crosswise into strips about ½-inch wide. Sprinkle with salt and pepper to taste.
2. Beat together egg and milk in a shallow dish.
3. Place wheat flour in a second shallow dish.
4. In a third shallow dish, mix together panko, plain breadcrumbs, ½ tsp. salt, and ¼ tsp. pepper.
5. Preheat air fryer to 390°F.
6. Dip liver strips in flour, egg wash, and then breadcrumbs, pressing in coating slightly to make crumbs stick.
7. Cooking half the liver at a time, place strips in air fryer basket in a single layer, close but not touching. Cook at 390°F for 5 Mins. or until done to your preference.
8. Repeat step 7 to cook remaining liver.

Lamb Chops

Ingredients:

- 2 tsp. oil
- ½ tsp. ground rosemary
- ½ tsp. lemon juice
- 1 lb. lamb chops, approximately 1-inch thick
- salt and pepper
- cooking spray

Directions:

1. Mix the oil, rosemary, and lemon juice together and rub into all sides of the lamb chops. Season to taste with salt and pepper.
2. For best flavor, cover lamb chops and allow them to rest in the fridge for 20 minutes.
3. Spray air fryer basket with nonstick spray and place lamb chops in it.
4. Cook at 360°F for approximately 20minutes. This will cook chops to medium. The meat will be juicy but have no remaining pink. Cook for a minute or two longer for well done chops. For rare chops, stop cooking after about 12minutes and check for doneness.

Better-than-chinese-take-out Sesame Beef

🍜 Servings: 4	🍲 Cooking Time: 14 Mins.

Ingredients:

- 1¼ lb. Beef flank steak
- 2½ tbsp. Regular or low-sodium soy sauce or gluten-free tamari sauce
- 2 tbsp. Toasted sesame oil
- 2½ tsp. Cornstarch
- 1 lb. 2 oz. (about 4½ cups) Frozen mixed vegetables for stir-fry, thawed, seasoning packet discarded
- 3 tbsp. Unseasoned rice vinegar (see here)
- 3 tbsp. Thai sweet chili sauce
- 2 tbsp. Light brown sugar
- 2 tbsp. White sesame seeds
- 2 tsp. Water
- Vegetable oil spray
- 1½ tbsp. Minced peeled fresh ginger
- 1 tbsp. Minced garlic

Directions:

1. Set the flank steak on a cutting board and run your clean fingers across it to figure out which way the meat's fibers are running. (Usually, they run the long way from end to end, or perhaps slightly at an angle lengthwise along the cut.) Cut the flank steak into three pieces parallel to the meat's grain. Then cut each of these pieces into ½-inch-wide strips against the grain.

2. Put the meat strips in a large bowl. For a small batch, add 2 tsp. of the soy or tamari sauce, 2 tsp. of the sesame oil, and ½ tsp. of the cornstarch; for a medium batch, add 1 tbsp. of the soy or tamari sauce, 1 tbsp. of the sesame oil, and 1 tsp. of the cornstarch; and for a large batch, add 1½ tbsp. of the soy or tamari sauce, 1½ tbsp. of the sesame oil, and 1½ tsp. of the cornstarch. Toss well until the meat is thoroughly coated in the marinade. Set aside at room temperature.

3. Preheat the air fryer to 400°F.

4. When the machine is at temperature, place the beef strips in the basket in as close to one layer as possible. The strips will overlap or even cover each other. Air-fry for 10 minutes, tossing and rearranging the strips three times so that the covered parts get exposed, until browned and even a little crisp. Pour the strips into a clean bowl.

5. Spread the vegetables in the basket and air-fry undisturbed for 4 minutes, just until they are heated through

and somewhat softened. Pour these into the bowl with the meat strips. Turn off the air fryer.

6. Whisk the rice vinegar, sweet chili sauce, brown sugar, sesame seeds, the remaining soy sauce, and the remaining sesame oil in a small bowl until well combined. For a small batch, whisk the remaining 1 tsp. cornstarch with the water in a second small bowl to make a smooth slurry; for medium batch, whisk the remaining 1½ tsp. cornstarch with the water in a second small bowl to make a smooth slurry; and for a large batch, whisk the remaining 2 tsp. cornstarch with the water in a second small bowl to make a smooth slurry.

7. Generously coat the inside of a large wok with vegetable oil spray, then set the wok over high heat for a few minutes. Add the ginger and garlic; stir-fry for 10 seconds or so, just until fragrant. Add the meat and vegetables; stir-fry for 1 minute to heat through.

8. Add the rice vinegar mixture and continue stir-frying until the sauce is bubbling, less than 1 minute. Add the cornstarch slurry and stir-fry until the sauce has thickened, just a few seconds. Remove the wok from the heat and serve hot.

Tonkatsu

Ingredients:

- ½ C. All-purpose flour or tapioca flour
- 1 Large egg white(s), well beaten
- ¾ C. Plain panko bread crumbs (gluten-free, if a concern)
- 3 4-ounce center-cut boneless pork loin chops (about ½ inch thick)
- Vegetable oil spray

Directions:

1. Preheat the air fryer to 375°F .

2. Set up and fill three shallow soup plates or small pie plates on your counter: one for the flour, one for the beaten egg white(s), and one for the bread crumbs.

3. Set a chop in the flour and roll it to coat all sides, even the ends. Gently shake off any excess flour and set it in the egg white(s). Gently roll and turn it to coat all sides. Let any excess egg white slip back into the rest, then set the chop in the bread crumbs. Turn it several times, pressing gently to get an even coating on all sides and the ends. Generously coat the breaded chop with vegetable oil spray, then set it aside so you can dredge, coat, and spray the remaining chop(s).

4. Set the chops in the basket with as much air space between them as possible. Air-fry undisturbed for 10 minutes, or until golden brown and crisp.

5. Use kitchen tongs to transfer the chops to a wire rack and cool for a couple of Mins. before serving.

Pizza Tortilla Rolls

 Servings: 4   **Cooking Time: 8 Mins.**

Ingredients:

- 1 tsp. butter
- ½ medium onion, slivered
- ½ red or green bell pepper, julienned
- 4 oz. fresh white mushrooms, chopped
- 8 flour tortillas (6- or 7-inch size)
- ½ C. pizza sauce
- 8 thin slices deli ham
- 24 pepperoni slices (about 1½ ounces)
- 1 C. shredded mozzarella cheese (about 4 ounces)
- oil for misting or cooking spray

Directions:

1. Place butter, onions, bell pepper, and mushrooms in air fryer baking pan. Cook at 390°F for 3minutes. Stir and cook 4 Mins. longer until just crisp and tender. Remove pan and set aside.

2. To assemble rolls, spread about 2 tsp. of pizza sauce on one half of each tortilla. Top with a slice of ham and 3 slices of pepperoni. Divide sautéed vegetables among tortillas and top with cheese.

3. Roll up tortillas, secure with toothpicks if needed, and spray with oil.

4. Place 4 rolls in air fryer basket and cook for 4minutes. Turn and cook 4 minutes, until heated through and lightly browned.

5. Repeat step 4 to cook remaining pizza rolls.

FISH AND SEAFOOD RECIPES

Potato-wrapped Salmon Fillets

🍲 **Servings: 3**   🍲 **Cooking Time: 8 Mins.**

Ingredients:

- 1 Large 1-pound elongated yellow potato(es), peeled
- 3 6-ounce, 1½-inch-wide, quite thick skinless salmon fillets
- Olive oil spray
- ¼ tsp. Table salt
- ¼ tsp. Ground black pepper

Directions:

1. Preheat the air fryer to 400°F.
2. Use a vegetable peeler or mandoline to make long strips from the potato(es). You'll need anywhere from 8 to 12 strips per fillet, depending on the shape of the potato and of the salmon fillet.
3. Drape potato strips over a salmon fillet, overlapping the strips to create an even "crust." Tuck the potato strips under the fillet, overlapping the strips underneath to create as smooth a bottom as you can. Wrap the remaining fillet(s) in the same way.
4. Gently turn the fillets over. Generously coat the bottoms with olive oil spray. Turn them back seam side down and generously coat the tops with the oil spray. Sprinkle the salt and pepper over the wrapped fillets.
5. Use a nonstick-safe spatula to gently transfer the fillets seam side down to the basket. It helps to remove the basket from the machine and set it on your work surface (keeping in mind that the basket's hot). Leave as much air space as possible between the fillets. Air-fry undisturbed for 8 minutes, or until golden brown and crisp.
6. Use a nonstick-safe spatula to gently transfer the fillets to serving plates. Cool for a couple of Mins. before serving.

Fish Tacos With Jalapeño-lime Sauce

🥣 **Servings: 4**   🍲 **Cooking Time: 7 Mins.**

Ingredients:

- Fish Tacos
- 1 lb. fish fillets
- ¼ tsp. cumin
- ¼ tsp. coriander
- ⅛ tsp. ground red pepper
- 1 tbsp. lime zest
- ¼ tsp. smoked paprika
- 1 tsp. oil
- cooking spray
- 6–8 corn or flour tortillas (6-inch size)
- Jalapeño-Lime Sauce

- ½ C. sour cream
- 1 tbsp. lime juice
- ¼ tsp. grated lime zest
- ½ tsp. minced jalapeño (flesh only)
- ¼ tsp. cumin
- Napa Cabbage Garnish
- 1 C. shredded Napa cabbage
- ¼ C. slivered red or green bell pepper
- ¼ C. slivered onion

Directions:

1. Slice the fish fillets into strips approximately ½-inch thick.
2. Put the strips into a sealable plastic bag along with the cumin, coriander, red pepper, lime zest, smoked paprika, and oil. Massage seasonings into the fish until evenly distributed.
3. Spray air fryer basket with nonstick cooking spray and place seasoned fish inside.
4. Cook at 390°F for approximately 5minutes. Shake basket to distribute fish. Cook an additional 2 minutes, until fish flakes easily.
5. While the fish is cooking, prepare the Jalapeño-Lime Sauce by mixing the sour cream, lime juice, lime zest, jalapeño, and cumin together to make a smooth sauce. Set aside.
6. Mix the cabbage, bell pepper, and onion together and set aside.
7. To warm refrigerated tortillas, wrap in damp paper towels and microwave for 30 to 60 seconds.
8. To serve, spoon some of fish into a warm tortilla. Add one or two tbsp. Napa Cabbage Garnish and drizzle with Jalapeño-Lime Sauce.

Easy Scallops With Lemon Butter

🥣 Servings: 3   🍲 Cooking Time: 4 Mins.

Ingredients:

- 1 tbsp. Olive oil
- 2 tsp. Minced garlic
- 1 tsp. Finely grated lemon zest
- ½ tsp. Red pepper flakes
- ¼ tsp. Table salt
- 1 lb. Sea scallops
- 3 tbsp. Butter, melted
- 1½ tbsp. Lemon juice

Directions:

1. Preheat the air fryer to 400°F.

2. Gently stir the olive oil, garlic, lemon zest, red pepper flakes, and salt in a bowl. Add the scallops and stir very gently until they are evenly and well coated.

3. When the machine is at temperature, arrange the scallops in a single layer in the basket. Some may touch. Air-fry undisturbed for 4 minutes, or until the scallops are opaque and firm.

4. While the scallops cook, stir the melted butter and lemon juice in a serving bowl. When the scallops are ready, pour them from the basket into this bowl. Toss well before serving.

Beer-breaded Halibut Fish Tacos

Servings: 4   **Cooking Time: 10 Mins.**

Ingredients:

- 1 lb. halibut, cut into 1-inch strips
- 1 C. light beer
- 1 jalapeño, minced and divided
- 1 clove garlic, minced
- ¼ tsp. ground cumin
- ½ C. cornmeal
- ¼ C. all-purpose flour
- 1¼ tsp. sea salt, divided
- 2 C. shredded cabbage
- 1 lime, juiced and divided
- ¼ C. Greek yogurt
- ¼ C. mayonnaise
- 1 C. grape tomatoes, quartered
- ½ C. chopped cilantro
- ¼ C. chopped onion
- 1 egg, whisked
- 8 corn tortillas

Directions:

1. In a shallow baking dish, place the fish, the beer, 1 tsp. of the minced jalapeño, the garlic, and the cumin. Cover and refrigerate for 30 minutes.
2. Meanwhile, in a medium bowl, mix together the cornmeal, flour, and ½ tsp. of the salt.
3. In large bowl, mix together the shredded cabbage, 1 tbsp. of the lime juice, the Greek yogurt, the mayonnaise, and ½ tsp. of the salt.
4. In a small bowl, make the pico de gallo by mixing together the tomatoes, cilantro, onion, ¼ tsp. of the salt, the remaining jalapeño, and the remaining lime juice.
5. Remove the fish from the refrigerator and discard the marinade. Dredge the fish in the whisked egg; then dredge the fish in the cornmeal flour mixture, until all pieces of fish have been breaded.
6. Preheat the air fryer to 350°F.
7. Place the fish in the air fryer basket and spray liberally with cooking spray. Cook for 6 minutes, flip and shake the fish, and cook another 4 minutes.
8. While the fish is cooking, heat the tortillas in a heavy skillet for 1 to 2 Mins. over high heat.
9. To assemble the tacos, place the battered fish on the heated tortillas, and top with slaw and pico de gallo. Serve immediately.

Crunchy And Buttery Cod With Ritz® Cracker Crust

🍽 Servings: 2	🍲 Cooking Time: 10 Mins.

Ingredients:

- ♦ 4 tbsp. butter, melted
- ♦ 8 to 10 RITZ® crackers, crushed into crumbs
- ♦ 2 (6-ounce) cod fillets
- ♦ salt and freshly ground black pepper
- ♦ 1 lemon

Directions:

1. Preheat the air fryer to 380°F.

2. Melt the butter in a small saucepan on the stovetop or in a microwavable dish in the microwave, and then transfer the butter to a shallow dish. Place the crushed RITZ® crackers into a second shallow dish.

3. Season the fish fillets with salt and freshly ground black pepper. Dip them into the butter and then coat both sides with the RITZ® crackers.

4. Place the fish into the air fryer basket and air-fry at 380°F for 10 minutes, flipping the fish over halfway through the cooking time.

5. Serve with a wedge of lemon to squeeze over the top.

Lobster Tails With Lemon Garlic Butter

🥣 Servings: 2	🍲 Cooking Time: 5 Mins.

Ingredients:

- 4 oz. unsalted butter
- 1 tbsp. finely chopped lemon zest
- 1 clove garlic, thinly sliced
- 2 (6-ounce) lobster tails
- salt and freshly ground black pepper
- ½ C. white wine
- ½ lemon, sliced
- vegetable oil

Directions:

1. Start by making the lemon garlic butter. Combine the butter, lemon zest and garlic in a small saucepan. Melt and simmer the butter on the stovetop over the lowest possible heat while you prepare the lobster tails.

2. Prepare the lobster tails by cutting down the middle of the top of the shell. Crack the bottom shell by squeezing the sides of the lobster together so that you can access the lobster meat inside. Pull the lobster tail up out of the shell, but leave it attached at the base of the tail. Lay the lobster meat on top of the shell and season with salt and freshly ground black pepper. Pour a little of the lemon garlic butter on top of the lobster meat and transfer the lobster to the refrigerator so that the butter solidifies a little.

3. Pour the white wine into the air fryer drawer and add the lemon slices. Preheat the air fryer to 400°F for 5 minutes.

4. Transfer the lobster tails to the air fryer basket. Air-fry at 370° for 5 minutes, brushing more butter on halfway through cooking. (Add a minute or two if your lobster tail is more than 6-ounces.) Remove and serve with more butter for dipping or drizzling.

Butternut Squash–wrapped Halibut Fillets

🥣 Servings: 3	🍲 Cooking Time: 11 Mins.

Ingredients:

- 15 Long spiralized peeled and seeded butternut squash strands
- 3 5- to 6-ounce skinless halibut fillets
- 3 tbsp. Butter, melted
- ¾ tsp. Mild paprika
- ¾ tsp. Table salt
- ¾ tsp. Ground black pepper

Directions:

1. Preheat the air fryer to 375°F .

2. Hold 5 long butternut squash strands together and wrap them around a fillet. Set it aside and wrap any remaining fillet(s).

3. Mix the melted butter, paprika, salt, and pepper in a small bowl. Brush this mixture over the squash-wrapped fillets on all sides.

4. When the machine is at temperature, set the fillets in the basket with as much air space between them as possible. Air-fry undisturbed for 10 minutes, or until the squash strands have browned but not burned. If the machine is at 360°F, you may need to add 1 minute to the cooking time. In any event, watch the fish carefully after the 8-minute mark.

5. Use a nonstick-safe spatula to gently transfer the fillets to a serving platter or plates. Cool for only a minute or so before serving.

Maple-crusted Salmon

Servings: 2　　**Cooking Time: 8 Mins.**

Ingredients:

- 12 oz. salmon filets
- ⅓ C. maple syrup
- 1 tsp. Worcestershire sauce
- 2 tsp. Dijon mustard or brown mustard
- ½ C. finely chopped walnuts
- ½ tsp. sea salt
- ½ lemon
- 1 tbsp. chopped parsley, for garnish

Directions:

1. Place the salmon in a shallow baking dish. Top with maple syrup, Worcestershire sauce, and mustard. Refrigerate for 30 minutes.
2. Preheat the air fryer to 350°F.
3. Remove the salmon from the marinade and discard the marinade.
4. Place the chopped nuts on top of the salmon filets, and sprinkle salt on top of the nuts. Place the salmon, skin side down, in the air fryer basket. Cook for 6 to 8 Mins. or until the fish flakes in the center.
5. Remove the salmon and plate on a serving platter. Squeeze fresh lemon over the top of the salmon and top with chopped parsley. Serve immediately.

Tuna Patties With Dill Sauce

Servings: 6　　　**Cooking Time: 10 Mins.**

Ingredients:

♦ Two 5-ounce cans albacore tuna, drained

♦ ½ tsp. garlic powder

♦ 2 tsp. dried dill, divided

♦ ½ tsp. black pepper

♦ ½ tsp. salt, divided

♦ ¼ C. minced onion

♦ 1 large egg

♦ 7 tbsp. mayonnaise, divided

♦ ¼ C. panko breadcrumbs

♦ 1 tsp. fresh lemon juice

♦ ¼ tsp. fresh lemon zest

♦ 6 pieces butterleaf lettuce

♦ 1 C. diced tomatoes

Directions:

1. In a large bowl, mix the tuna with the garlic powder, 1 tsp. of the dried dill, the black pepper, ¼ tsp. of the salt, and the onion. Make sure to use the back of a fork to really break up the tuna so there are no large chunks.

2. Mix in the egg and 1 tbsp. of the mayonnaise; then fold in the breadcrumbs so the tuna begins to form a thick batter that holds together.

3. Portion the tuna mixture into 6 equal patties and place on a plate lined with parchment paper in the refrigerator for at least 30 minutes. This will help the patties hold together in the air fryer.

4. When ready to cook, preheat the air fryer to 350°F.

5. Liberally spray the metal trivet that sits inside the air fryer basket with olive oil mist and place the patties onto the trivet.

6. Cook for 5 minutes, flip, and cook another 5 minutes.

7. While the patties are cooking, make the dill sauce by combining the remaining 6 tbsp. of mayonnaise with the remaining 1 tsp. of dill, the lemon juice, the lemon zest, and the remaining ¼ tsp. of salt. Set aside.

8. Remove the patties from the air fryer.

9. Place 1 slice of lettuce on a plate and top with the tuna patty and a tomato slice. Repeat to form the remaining servings. Drizzle the dill dressing over the top. Serve immediately.

POULTRY RECIPES

Italian Roasted Chicken Thighs

🍜 Servings: 6	🍲 Cooking Time: 14 Mins.

Ingredients:

- 6 boneless chicken thighs
- ½ tsp. dried oregano
- ½ tsp. garlic powder
- ½ tsp. sea salt
- ½ tsp. black pepper
- ¼ tsp. crushed red pepper flakes

Directions:

1. Pat the chicken thighs with paper towel.
2. In a small bowl, mix the oregano, garlic powder, salt, pepper, and crushed red pepper flakes. Rub the spice mixture onto the chicken thighs.
3. Preheat the air fryer to 400°F.
4. Place the chicken thighs in the air fryer basket and spray with cooking spray. Cook for 10 minutes, turn over, and cook another 4 minutes. When cooking completes, the internal temperature should read 165°F.

Chicken Fried Steak With Gravy

🍲 Servings: 4	🍲 Cooking Time: 10 Mins.

Ingredients:

- ½ C. flour
- 2 tsp. salt, divided
- freshly ground black pepper
- ¼ tsp. garlic powder
- 1 C. buttermilk
- 1 C. fine breadcrumbs
- 4 tenderized top round steaks (about 6 to 8 oz. each; ½-inch thick)
- vegetable or canola oil
- For the Gravy:

- 2 tbsp. butter or bacon drippings
- ¼ onion, minced (about ¼ cup)
- 1 clove garlic, smashed
- ¼ tsp. dried thyme
- 3 tbsp. flour
- 1 C. milk
- salt and lots of freshly ground black pepper
- a few dashes of Worcestershire sauce

Directions:

1. Set up a dredging station. Combine the flour, 1 tsp. of salt, black pepper and garlic powder in a shallow bowl. Pour the buttermilk into a second shallow bowl. Finally, put the breadcrumbs and 1 tsp. of salt in a third shallow bowl.

2. Dip the tenderized steaks into the flour, then the buttermilk, and then the breadcrumb mixture, pressing the crumbs onto the steak. Place them on a baking sheet and spray both sides generously with vegetable or canola oil.

3. Preheat the air fryer to 400°F.

4. Transfer the steaks to the air fryer basket, two at a time, and air-fry for 10 minutes, flipping the steaks over halfway through the cooking time. This will cook your steaks to medium. If you want the steaks cooked a little more or less, add or subtract a minute or two. Hold the first batch of steaks warm in a 170°F oven while you cook the second batch.

5. While the steaks are cooking, make the gravy. Melt the butter in a small saucepan over medium heat on the stovetop. Add the onion, garlic and thyme and cook for five minutes, until the onion is soft and just starting to brown. Stir in the flour and cook for another five minutes, stirring regularly, until the mixture starts to brown. Whisk in the milk and bring the mixture to a boil to thicken. Season to taste with salt, lots of freshly ground black pepper and a few dashes of Worcestershire sauce.

6. Plate the chicken fried steaks with mashed potatoes and vegetables and serve the gravy at the table to pour over the top.

Buffalo Egg Rolls

🍜 Servings: 8	🍲 Cooking Time: 9 Mins.

Ingredients:

- 1 tsp. water
- 1 tbsp. cornstarch
- 1 egg
- 2½ C. cooked chicken, diced or shredded (see opposite page)
- ⅓ C. chopped green onion
- ⅓ C. diced celery
- ⅓ C. buffalo wing sauce
- 8 egg roll wraps
- oil for misting or cooking spray
- Blue Cheese Dip
- 3 oz. cream cheese, softened
- ⅓ C. blue cheese, crumbled
- 1 tsp. Worcestershire sauce
- ¼ tsp. garlic powder
- ¼ C. buttermilk (or sour cream)

Directions:

1. Mix water and cornstarch in a small bowl until dissolved. Add egg, beat well, and set aside.
2. In a medium size bowl, mix together chicken, green onion, celery, and buffalo wing sauce.
3. Divide chicken mixture evenly among 8 egg roll wraps, spooning ½ inch from one edge.
4. Moisten all edges of each wrap with beaten egg wash.
5. Fold the short ends over filling, then roll up tightly and press to seal edges.
6. Brush outside of wraps with egg wash, then spritz with oil or cooking spray.
7. Place 4 egg rolls in air fryer basket.
8. Cook at 390°F for 9minutes or until outside is brown and crispy.
9. While the rolls are cooking, prepare the Blue Cheese Dip. With a fork, mash together cream cheese and blue cheese.
10. Stir in remaining ingredients.
11. Dip should be just thick enough to slightly cling to egg rolls. If too thick, stir in buttermilk or milk 1 tbsp. at a time until you reach the desired consistency.
12. Cook remaining 4 egg rolls as in steps 7 and 8.
13. Serve while hot with Blue Cheese Dip, more buffalo wing sauce, or both.

Maple Bacon Wrapped Chicken Breasts

Servings: 2   **Cooking Time: 18 Mins.**

Ingredients:

- 2 (6-ounce) boneless, skinless chicken breasts
- 2 tbsp. maple syrup, divided
- freshly ground black pepper
- 6 slices thick-sliced bacon
- fresh celery or parsley leaves
- Ranch Dressing:
- ¼ C. mayonnaise
- ¼ C. buttermilk
- ¼ C. Greek yogurt
- 1 tbsp. chopped fresh chives
- 1 tbsp. chopped fresh parsley
- 1 tbsp. chopped fresh dill
- 1 tbsp. lemon juice
- salt and freshly ground black pepper

Directions:

1. Brush the chicken breasts with half the maple syrup and season with freshly ground black pepper. Wrap three slices of bacon around each chicken breast, securing the ends with toothpicks.
2. Preheat the air fryer to 380°F.
3. Air-fry the chicken for 6 minutes. Then turn the chicken breasts over, pour more maple syrup on top and air-fry for another 6 minutes. Turn the chicken breasts one more time, brush the remaining maple syrup all over and continue to air-fry for a final 6 minutes.
4. While the chicken is cooking, prepare the dressing by combining all the dressing ingredients together in a bowl.
5. When the chicken has finished cooking, remove the toothpicks and serve each breast with a little dressing drizzled over each one. Scatter lots of fresh celery or parsley leaves on top.

Asian Meatball Tacos

Ingredients:

- 1 lb. lean ground turkey
- 3 tbsp. soy sauce
- 1 tbsp. brown sugar
- ½ tsp. onion powder
- ½ tsp. garlic powder
- 1 tbsp. sesame seeds
- 1 English cucumber
- 4 radishes
- 2 tbsp. white wine vinegar
- 1 lime, juiced and divided
- 1 tbsp. avocado oil
- Salt, to taste
- ½ C. Greek yogurt
- 1 to 3 tsp. Sriracha, based on desired spiciness
- 1 C. shredded cabbage
- ¼ C. chopped cilantro
- Eight 6-inch flour tortillas

Directions:

1. Preheat the air fryer to 360°F.
2. In a large bowl, mix the ground turkey, soy sauce, brown sugar, onion powder, garlic powder, and sesame seeds. Form the meat into 1-inch meatballs and place in the air fryer basket. Cook for 5 minutes, shake the basket, and cook another 5 minutes. Using a food thermometer, make sure the internal temperature of the meatballs is 165°F.
3. Meanwhile, dice the cucumber and radishes and place in a medium bowl. Add the white wine vinegar, 1 tsp. of the lime juice, and the avocado oil, and stir to coat. Season with salt to desired taste.
4. In a large bowl, mix the Greek yogurt, Sriracha, and the remaining lime juice, and stir. Add in the cabbage and cilantro; toss well to create a slaw.
5. In a heavy skillet, heat the tortillas over medium heat for 1 to 2 Mins. on each side, or until warmed.
6. To serve, place a tortilla on a plate, top with 5 meatballs, then with cucumber and radish salad, and finish with 2 tbsp. of cabbage slaw.

Simple Buttermilk Fried Chicken

🍲 Servings: 4	🍲 Cooking Time: 27 Mins.

Ingredients:

- 1 (4-pound) chicken, cut into 8 pieces
- 2 C. buttermilk
- hot sauce (optional)
- 1½ C. flour
- 2 tsp. paprika
- 1 tsp. salt
- freshly ground black pepper
- 2 eggs, lightly beaten
- vegetable oil, in a spray bottle

Directions:

1. Cut the chicken into 8 pieces and submerge them in the buttermilk and hot sauce, if using. A zipper-sealable plastic bag works well for this. Let the chicken soak in the buttermilk for at least one hour or even overnight in the refrigerator.

2. Set up a dredging station. Mix the flour, paprika, salt and black pepper in a clean zipper-sealable plastic bag. Whisk the eggs and place them in a shallow dish. Remove four pieces of chicken from the buttermilk and transfer them to the bag with the flour. Shake them around to coat on all sides. Remove the chicken from the flour, shaking off any excess flour, and dip them into the beaten egg. Return the chicken to the bag of seasoned flour and shake again. Set the coated chicken aside and repeat with the remaining four pieces of chicken.

3. Preheat the air fryer to 370°F.

4. Spray the chicken on all sides with the vegetable oil and then transfer one batch to the air fryer basket. Air-fry the chicken at 370°F for 20 minutes, flipping the pieces over halfway through the cooking process, taking care not to knock off the breading. Transfer the chicken to a plate, but do not cover. Repeat with the second batch of chicken.

5. Lower the temperature on the air fryer to 340°F. Flip the chicken back over and place the first batch of chicken on top of the second batch already in the basket. Air-fry for another 7 Mins. and serve warm.

Chicken Cutlets With Broccoli Rabe And Roasted Peppers

 Servings: 2　　　 **Cooking Time: 10 Mins.**

Ingredients:

- ½ bunch broccoli rabe
- olive oil, in a spray bottle
- salt and freshly ground black pepper
- ⅔ C. roasted red pepper strips
- 2 (4-ounce) boneless, skinless chicken breasts
- 2 tbsp. all-purpose flour
- 1 egg, beaten
- ⅓ C. seasoned breadcrumbs
- 2 slices aged provolone cheese

Directions:

1. Bring a medium saucepot of salted water to a boil on the stovetop. Blanch the broccoli rabe for 3 Mins. in the boiling water and then drain. When it has cooled a little, squeeze out as much water as possible, drizzle a little olive oil on top, season with salt and black pepper and set aside. Dry the roasted red peppers with a clean kitchen towel and set them aside as well.

2. Place each chicken breast between 2 pieces of plastic wrap. Use a meat pounder to flatten the chicken breasts to about ½-inch thick. Season the chicken on both sides with salt and pepper.

3. Preheat the air fryer to 400°F.

4. Set up a dredging station with three shallow dishes. Place the flour in one dish, the egg in a second dish and the breadcrumbs in a third dish. Coat the chicken on all sides with the flour. Shake off any excess flour and dip the chicken into the egg. Let the excess egg drip off and coat both sides of the chicken in the breadcrumbs. Spray the chicken with olive oil on both sides and transfer to the air fryer basket.

5. Air-fry the chicken at 400°F for 5 minutes. Turn the chicken over and air-fry for another minute. Then, top the chicken breast with the broccoli rabe and roasted peppers. Place a slice of the provolone cheese on top and secure it with a toothpick or two.

6. Air-fry at 360° for 3 to 4 Mins. to melt the cheese and warm everything together.

Parmesan Chicken Fingers

Servings: 2   **Cooking Time: 19 Mins.**

Ingredients:

- ½ C. flour
- 1 tsp. salt
- freshly ground black pepper
- 2 eggs, beaten
- ¾ C. seasoned panko breadcrumbs
- ¾ C. grated Parmesan cheese
- 8 chicken tenders (about 1 pound)
- OR
- 2 to 3 boneless, skinless chicken breasts, cut into strips
- vegetable oil
- marinara sauce

Directions:

1. Set up a dredging station. Combine the flour, salt and pepper in a shallow dish. Place the beaten eggs in second shallow dish, and combine the panko breadcrumbs and Parmesan cheese in a third shallow dish.

2. Dredge the chicken tenders in the flour mixture. Then dip them into the egg, and finally place the chicken in the breadcrumb mixture. Press the coating onto both sides of the chicken tenders. Place the coated chicken tenders on a baking sheet until they are all coated. Spray both sides of the chicken fingers with vegetable oil.

3. Preheat the air fryer to 360°F.

4. Air-fry the chicken fingers in two batches. Transfer half the chicken fingers to the air fryer basket and air-fry for 9 minutes, turning the chicken over halfway through the cooking time. When the second batch of chicken fingers has finished cooking, return the first batch to the air fryer with the second batch and air-fry for one minute to heat everything through.

5. Serve immediately with marinara sauce, honey-mustard, ketchup or your favorite dipping sauce.

Teriyaki Chicken Legs

Servings: 2   **Cooking Time: 20 Mins.**

Ingredients:

♦ 4 tbsp. teriyaki sauce

♦ 1 tbsp. orange juice

♦ 1 tsp. smoked paprika

♦ 4 chicken legs

♦ cooking spray

Directions:

1. Mix together the teriyaki sauce, orange juice, and smoked paprika. Brush on all sides of chicken legs.

2. Spray air fryer basket with nonstick cooking spray and place chicken in basket.

3. Cook at 360°F for 6minutes. Turn and baste with sauce. Cook for 6 moreminutes, turn and baste. Cook for 8 Mins. more, until juices run clear when chicken is pierced with a fork.

SANDWICHES AND BURGERS RECIPES

Inside Out Cheeseburgers

Servings: 2   **Cooking Time: 20 Mins.**

Ingredients:

- ¾ lb. lean ground beef
- 3 tbsp. minced onion
- 4 tsp. ketchup
- 2 tsp. yellow mustard
- salt and freshly ground black pepper
- 4 slices of Cheddar cheese, broken into smaller pieces
- 8 hamburger dill pickle chips

Directions:

1. Combine the ground beef, minced onion, ketchup, mustard, salt and pepper in a large bowl. Mix well to thoroughly combine the ingredients. Divide the meat into four equal portions.

2. To make the stuffed burgers, flatten each portion of meat into a thin patty. Place 4 pickle chips and half of the cheese onto the center of two of the patties, leaving a rim around the edge of the patty exposed. Place the remaining two patties on top of the first and press the meat together firmly, sealing the edges tightly. With the burgers on a flat surface, press the sides of the burger with the palm of your hand to create a straight edge. This will help keep the stuffing inside the burger while it cooks.

3. Preheat the air fryer to 370°F.

4. Place the burgers inside the air fryer basket and air-fry for 20 minutes, flipping the burgers over halfway through the cooking time.

5. Serve the cheeseburgers on buns with lettuce and tomato.

Provolone Stuffed Meatballs

Servings: 4   **Cooking Time: 12 Mins.**

Ingredients:

- 1 tbsp. olive oil
- 1 small onion, very finely chopped
- 1 to 2 cloves garlic, minced
- ¾ lb. ground beef
- ¾ lb. ground pork
- ¾ C. breadcrumbs
- ¼ C. grated Parmesan cheese
- ¼ C. finely chopped fresh parsley (or 1 tbsp. dried parsley)
- ½ tsp. dried oregano
- 1½ tsp. salt
- freshly ground black pepper
- 2 eggs, lightly beaten
- 5 oz. sharp or aged provolone cheese, cut into 1-inch cubes

Directions:

1. Preheat a skillet over medium-high heat. Add the oil and cook the onion and garlic until tender, but not browned.

2. Transfer the onion and garlic to a large bowl and add the beef, pork, breadcrumbs, Parmesan cheese, parsley, oregano, salt, pepper and eggs. Mix well until all the ingredients are combined. Divide the mixture into 12 evenly sized balls. Make one meatball at a time, by pressing a hole in the meatball mixture with your finger and pushing a piece of provolone cheese into the hole. Mold the meat back into a ball, enclosing the cheese.

3. Preheat the air fryer to 380°F.

4. Working in two batches, transfer six of the meatballs to the air fryer basket and air-fry for 12 minutes, shaking the basket and turning the meatballs a couple of times during the cooking process. Repeat with the remaining six meatballs. You can pop the first batch of meatballs into the air fryer for the last two Mins. of cooking to re-heat them. Serve warm.

Black Bean Veggie Burgers

🍲 Servings: 3   🍲 Cooking Time: 10 Mins.

Ingredients:

- 1 C. Drained and rinsed canned black beans
- ⅓ C. Pecan pieces
- ⅓ C. Rolled oats (not quick-cooking or steel-cut; gluten-free, if a concern)
- 2 tbsp. (or 1 small egg) Pasteurized egg substitute, such as Egg Beaters (gluten-free, if a concern)
- 2 tsp. Red ketchup-like chili sauce, such as Heinz
- ¼ tsp. Ground cumin
- ¼ tsp. Dried oregano
- ¼ tsp. Table salt
- ¼ tsp. Ground black pepper
- Olive oil
- Olive oil spray

Directions:

1. Preheat the air fryer to 400°F.

2. Put the beans, pecans, oats, egg substitute or egg, chili sauce, cumin, oregano, salt, and pepper in a food processor. Cover and process to a coarse paste that will hold its shape like sugar-cookie dough, adding olive oil in 1-teaspoon increments to get the mixture to blend smoothly. The amount of olive oil is actually dependent on the internal moisture content of the beans and the oats. Figure on about 1 tbsp. (three 1-teaspoon additions) for the smaller batch, with proportional increases for the other batches. A little too much olive oil can't hurt, but a dry paste will fall apart as it cooks and a far-too-wet paste will stick to the basket.

3. Scrape down and remove the blade. Using clean, wet hands, form the paste into two 4-inch patties for the small batch, three 4-inch patties for the medium, or four 4-inch patties for the large batch, setting them one by one on a cutting board. Generously coat both sides of the patties with olive oil spray.

4. Set them in the basket in one layer. Air-fry undisturbed for 10 minutes, or until lightly browned and crisp at the edges.

5. Use a nonstick-safe spatula, and perhaps a flatware fork for balance, to transfer the burgers to a wire rack. Cool for 5 Mins. before serving.

Sausage And Pepper Heros

Servings: 3   **Cooking Time: 11 Mins.**

Ingredients:

♦ 3 links (about 9 oz. total) Sweet Italian sausages (gluten-free, if a concern)

♦ 1½ Medium red or green bell pepper(s), stemmed, cored, and cut into ½-inch-wide strips

♦ 1 medium Yellow or white onion(s), peeled, halved, and sliced into thin half-moons

♦ 3 Long soft rolls, such as hero, hoagie, or Italian sub rolls (gluten-free, if a concern), split open lengthwise

♦ For garnishing Balsamic vinegar

♦ For garnishing Fresh basil leaves

Directions:

1. Preheat the air fryer to 400°F.

2. When the machine is at temperature, set the sausage links in the basket in one layer and air-fry undisturbed for 5 minutes.

3. Add the pepper strips and onions. Continue air-frying, tossing and rearranging everything about once every minute, for 5 minutes, or until the sausages are browned and an instant-read meat thermometer inserted into one of the links registers 160°F.

4. Use a nonstick-safe spatula and kitchen tongs to transfer the sausages and vegetables to a cutting board. Set the rolls cut side down in the basket in one layer (working in batches as necessary) and air-fry undisturbed for 1 minute, to toast the rolls a bit and warm them up. Set 1 sausage with some pepper strips and onions in each warm roll, sprinkle balsamic vinegar over the sandwich fillings, and garnish with basil leaves.

Chicken Spiedies

Ingredients:

- 1¼ lb. Boneless skinless chicken thighs, trimmed of any fat blobs and cut into 2-inch pieces
- 3 tbsp. Red wine vinegar
- 2 tbsp. Olive oil
- 2 tbsp. Minced fresh mint leaves
- 2 tbsp. Minced fresh parsley leaves
- 2 tsp. Minced fresh dill fronds
- ¾ tsp. Fennel seeds
- ¾ tsp. Table salt
- Up to a ¼ tsp. Red pepper flakes
- 3 Long soft rolls, such as hero, hoagie, or Italian sub rolls (gluten-free, if a concern), split open lengthwise
- 4½ tbsp. Regular or low-fat mayonnaise (not fat-free; gluten-free, if a concern)
- 1½ tbsp. Distilled white vinegar
- 1½ tsp. Ground black pepper

Directions:

1. Mix the chicken, vinegar, oil, mint, parsley, dill, fennel seeds, salt, and red pepper flakes in a zip-closed plastic bag. Seal, gently massage the marinade ingredients into the meat, and refrigerate for at least 2 hours or up to 6 hours. (Longer than that and the meat can turn rubbery.)

2. Set the plastic bag out on the counter (to make the contents a little less frigid). Preheat the air fryer to 400°F.

3. When the machine is at temperature, use kitchen tongs to set the chicken thighs in the basket (discard any remaining marinade) and air-fry undisturbed for 6 minutes. Turn the thighs over and continue air-frying undisturbed for 6 Mins. more, until well browned, cooked through, and even a little crunchy.

4. Dump the contents of the basket onto a wire rack and cool for 2 or 3 minutes. Divide the chicken evenly between the rolls. Whisk the mayonnaise, vinegar, and black pepper in a small bowl until smooth. Drizzle this sauce over the chicken pieces in the rolls.

Chicken Club Sandwiches

Servings: 3   **Cooking Time: 15 Mins.**

Ingredients:

♦ 3 5- to 6-ounce boneless skinless chicken breasts

♦ 6 Thick-cut bacon strips (gluten-free, if a concern)

♦ 3 Long soft rolls, such as hero, hoagie, or Italian sub rolls (gluten-free, if a concern)

♦ 3 tbsp. Regular, low-fat, or fat-free mayonnaise (gluten-free, if a concern)

♦ 3 Lettuce leaves, preferably romaine or iceberg

♦ 6 ¼-inch-thick tomato slices

Directions:

1. Preheat the air fryer to 375°F .

2. Wrap each chicken breast with 2 strips of bacon, spiraling the bacon around the meat, slightly overlapping the strips on each revolution. Start the second strip of bacon farther down the breast but on a line with the start of the first strip so they both end at a lined-up point on the chicken breast.

3. When the machine is at temperature, set the wrapped breasts bacon-seam side down in the basket with space between them. Air-fry undisturbed for 12 minutes, until the bacon is browned, crisp, and cooked through and an instant-read meat thermometer inserted into the center of a breast registers 165°F. You may need to add 2 Mins. in the air fryer if the temperature is at 360°F.

4. Use kitchen tongs to transfer the breasts to a wire rack. Split the rolls open lengthwise and set them cut side down in the basket. Air-fry for 1 minute, or until warmed through.

5. Use kitchen tongs to transfer the rolls to a cutting board. Spread 1 tbsp. mayonnaise on the cut side of one half of each roll. Top with a chicken breast, lettuce leaf, and tomato slice. Serve warm.

Reuben Sandwiches

Servings: 2　　　Cooking Time: 11 Mins.

Ingredients:

- ½ lb. Sliced deli corned beef
- 4 tsp. Regular or low-fat mayonnaise (not fat-free)
- 4 Rye bread slices
- 2 tbsp. plus 2 tsp. Russian dressing
- ½ C. Purchased sauerkraut, squeezed by the handful over the sink to get rid of excess moisture
- 2 oz. (2 to 4 slices) Swiss cheese slices (optional)

Directions:

1. Set the corned beef in the basket, slip the basket into the machine, and heat the air fryer to 400°F. Air-fry undisturbed for 3 Mins. from the time the basket is put in the machine, just to warm up the meat.

2. Use kitchen tongs to transfer the corned beef to a cutting board. Spread 1 tsp. mayonnaise on one side of each slice of rye bread, rubbing the mayonnaise into the bread with a small flatware knife.

3. Place the bread slices mayonnaise side down on a cutting board. Spread the Russian dressing over the "dry" side of each slice. For one sandwich, top one slice of bread with the corned beef, sauerkraut, and cheese (if using). For two sandwiches, top two slices of bread each with half of the corned beef, sauerkraut, and cheese (if using). Close the sandwiches with the remaining bread, setting it mayonnaise side up on top.

4. Set the sandwich(es) in the basket and air-fry undisturbed for 8 minutes, or until browned and crunchy.

5. Use a nonstick-safe spatula, and perhaps a flatware fork for balance, to transfer the sandwich(es) to a cutting board. Cool for 2 or 3 Mins. before slicing in half and serving.

Inside-out Cheeseburgers

Servings: 3　　　**Cooking Time: 9-11 Mins.**

Ingredients:

- 1 lb. 2 oz. 90% lean ground beef
- ¾ tsp. Dried oregano
- ¾ tsp. Table salt
- ¾ tsp. Ground black pepper
- ¼ tsp. Garlic powder
- 6 tbsp. (about 1½ ounces) Shredded Cheddar, Swiss, or other semi-firm cheese, or a purchased blend of shredded cheeses
- 3 Hamburger buns (gluten-free, if a concern), split open

Directions:

1. Preheat the air fryer to 375°F .
2. Gently mix the ground beef, oregano, salt, pepper, and garlic powder in a bowl until well combined without turning the mixture to mush. Form it into two 6-inch patties for the small batch, three for the medium, or four for the large.
3. Place 2 tbsp. of the shredded cheese in the center of each patty. With clean hands, fold the sides of the patty up to cover the cheese, then pick it up and roll it gently into a ball to seal the cheese inside. Gently press it back into a 5-inch burger without letting any cheese squish out. Continue filling and preparing more burgers, as needed.
4. Place the burgers in the basket in one layer and air-fry undisturbed for 8 Mins. for medium or 10 Mins. for well-done. (An instant-read meat thermometer won't work for these burgers because it will hit the mostly melted cheese inside and offer a hotter temperature than the surrounding meat.)
5. Use a nonstick-safe spatula, and perhaps a flatware fork for balance, to transfer the burgers to a cutting board. Set the buns cut side down in the basket in one layer (working in batches as necessary) and air-fry undisturbed for 1 minute, to toast a bit and warm up. Cool the burgers a few Mins. more, then serve them warm in the buns.

Lamb Burgers

🍜 Servings: 3	🍲 Cooking Time: 17 Mins.

Ingredients:

- 1 lb. 2 oz. Ground lamb
- 3 tbsp. Crumbled feta
- 1 tsp. Minced garlic
- 1 tsp. Tomato paste
- ¾ tsp. Ground coriander
- ¾ tsp. Ground dried ginger
- Up to ⅛ tsp. Cayenne
- Up to a ⅛ tsp. Table salt (optional)
- 3 Kaiser rolls or hamburger buns (gluten-free, if a concern), split open

Directions:

1. Preheat the air fryer to 375°F .
2. Gently mix the ground lamb, feta, garlic, tomato paste, coriander, ginger, cayenne, and salt (if using) in a bowl until well combined, trying to keep the bits of cheese intact. Form this mixture into two 5-inch patties for the small batch, three 5-inch patties for the medium, or four 5-inch patties for the large.
3. Set the patties in the basket in one layer and air-fry undisturbed for 16 minutes, or until an instant-read meat thermometer inserted into one burger registers 160°F. (The cheese is not an issue with the temperature probe in this recipe as it was for the Inside-Out Cheeseburgers, because the feta is so well mixed into the ground meat.)
4. Use a nonstick-safe spatula, and perhaps a flatware fork for balance, to transfer the burgers to a cutting board. Set the buns cut side down in the basket in one layer (working in batches as necessary) and air-fry undisturbed for 1 minute, to toast a bit and warm up. Serve the burgers warm in the buns.

APPETIZERS AND SNACKS

Parmesan Pizza Nuggets

Servings: 8   **Cooking Time: 6 Mins.**

Ingredients:

- ¾ C. warm filtered water
- 1 package fast-rising yeast
- ½ tsp. salt
- 2 C. all-purpose flour
- ¼ C. finely grated Parmesan cheese
- 1 tsp. Italian seasoning
- 2 tbsp. extra-virgin olive oil
- 1 tsp. kosher salt

Directions:

1. Preheat the air fryer to 370°F.
2. In a large microwave-safe bowl, add the water. Heat for 40 seconds in the microwave. Remove and mix in the yeast and salt. Let sit 5 minutes.
3. Meanwhile, in a medium bowl, mix the flour with the Parmesan cheese and Italian seasoning. Set aside.
4. Using a stand mixer with a dough hook attachment, add the yeast liquid and then mix in the flour mixture ⅓ C. at a time until all the flour mixture is added and a dough is formed.
5. Remove the bowl from the stand, and then let the dough rise for 1 hour in a warm space, covered with a kitchen towel.
6. After the dough has doubled in size, remove it from the bowl and punch it down a few times on a lightly floured flat surface.
7. Divide the dough into 4 balls, and then roll each ball out into a long, skinny, sticklike shape.
8. Using a sharp knife, cut each dough stick into 6 pieces. Repeat for the remaining dough balls until you have about 24 nuggets formed.
9. Lightly brush the top of each bite with the egg whites and cover with a pinch of sea salt.
10. Spray the air fryer basket with olive oil spray and place the pizza nuggets on top. Cook for 6 minutes, or until lightly browned. Remove and keep warm.
11. Repeat until all the nuggets are cooked.
12. Serve warm.

Crunchy Spicy Chickpeas

Ingredients:

- 2½ C. Canned chickpeas, drained and rinsed
- 2½ tbsp. Vegetable or canola oil
- up to 1 tbsp. Cajun or jerk dried seasoning blend (see here for a Cajun blend, here for a jerk blend)
- up to ¾ tsp. Table salt (optional)

Directions:

1. Preheat the air fryer to 400°F.

2. Toss the chickpeas, oil, seasoning blend, and salt (if using) in a large bowl until the chickpeas are evenly coated.

3. When the machine is at temperature, pour the chickpeas into the basket. Air-fry for 12 minutes, removing the basket at the 4- and 8-minute marks to toss and rearrange the chickpeas, until very aromatic and perhaps sizzling but not burned.

4. Pour the chickpeas into a large serving bowl. Cool for a couple of minutes, gently stirring once, before you dive in.

Cheesy Tortellini Bites

Servings: 8　　　**Cooking Time: 10 Mins.**

Ingredients:

- 1 large egg
- ½ tsp. black pepper
- ½ tsp. garlic powder
- 1 tsp. Italian seasoning
- 12 oz. frozen cheese tortellini
- ½ C. panko breadcrumbs

Directions:

1. Preheat the air fryer to 380°F.
2. Spray the air fryer basket with an olive-oil-based spray.
3. In a medium bowl, whisk the egg with the pepper, garlic powder, and Italian seasoning.
4. Dip the tortellini in the egg batter and then coat with the breadcrumbs. Place each tortellini in the basket, trying not to overlap them. You may need to cook in batches to ensure the even crisp all around.
5. Bake for 5 minutes, shake the basket, and bake another 5 minutes.
6. Remove and let cool 5 minutes. Serve with marinara sauce, ranch, or your favorite dressing.

Turkey Burger Sliders

🥣 Servings: 8	🍲 Cooking Time: 7 Mins.

Ingredients:

♦ 1 lb. ground turkey

♦ ¼ tsp. curry powder

♦ 1 tsp. Hoisin sauce

♦ ½ tsp. salt

♦ 8 slider buns

♦ ½ C. slivered red onions

♦ ½ C. slivered green or red bell pepper

♦ ½ C. fresh chopped pineapple (or pineapple tidbits from kids' fruit cups, drained)

♦ light cream cheese, softened

Directions:

1. Combine turkey, curry powder, Hoisin sauce, and salt and mix together well.

2. Shape turkey mixture into 8 small patties.

3. Place patties in air fryer basket and cook at 360°F for 7minutes, until patties are well done and juices run clear.

4. Place each patty on the bottom half of a slider bun and top with onions, peppers, and pineapple. Spread the remaining bun halves with cream cheese to taste, place on top, and serve.

Fried Pickles

Servings: 2   **Cooking Time: 15 Mins.**

Ingredients:

- 1 egg
- 1 tbsp. milk
- ¼ tsp. hot sauce
- 2 C. sliced dill pickles, well drained
- ¾ C. breadcrumbs
- oil for misting or cooking spray

Directions:

1. Preheat air fryer to 390°F.
2. Beat together egg, milk, and hot sauce in a bowl large enough to hold all the pickles.
3. Add pickles to the egg wash and stir well to coat.
4. Place breadcrumbs in a large plastic bag or container with lid.
5. Drain egg wash from pickles and place them in bag with breadcrumbs. Shake to coat.
6. Pile pickles into air fryer basket and spray with oil.
7. Cook for 5minutes. Shake basket and spray with oil.
8. Cook 5 more minutes. Shake and spray again. Separate any pickles that have stuck together and mist any spots you've missed.
9. Cook for 5minutes longer or until dark golden brown and crispy.

Buffalo Cauliflower

Ingredients:

- 1 large head of cauliflower, washed and cut into medium-size florets
- ½ C. all-purpose flour
- ¼ C. melted butter
- 3 tbsp. hot sauce
- ½ tsp. garlic powder
- ½ C. blue cheese dip or ranch dressing (optional)

Directions:

1. Preheat the air fryer to 350°F.
2. Make sure the cauliflower florets are dry, and then coat them in flour.
3. Liberally spray the air fryer basket with an olive oil mist. Place the cauliflower into the basket, making sure not to stack them on top of each other. Depending on the size of your air fryer, you may need to do this in two batches.
4. Cook for 6 minutes, then shake the basket, and cook another 6 minutes.
5. While cooking, mix the melted butter, hot sauce, and garlic powder in a large bowl.
6. Carefully remove the cauliflower from the air fryer. Toss the cauliflower into the butter mixture to coat. Repeat Steps 2–4 for any leftover cauliflower. Serve warm with the dip of your choice.

Cinnamon Apple Crisps

Servings: 1   **Cooking Time: 22 Mins.**

Ingredients:

- 1 large apple
- ½ tsp. ground cinnamon
- 2 tsp. avocado oil or coconut oil

Directions:

1. Preheat the air fryer to 300°F.
2. Using a mandolin or knife, slice the apples to ¼-inch thickness. Pat the apples dry with a paper towel or kitchen cloth. Sprinkle the apple slices with ground cinnamon. Spray or drizzle the oil over the top of the apple slices and toss to coat.
3. Place the apple slices in the air fryer basket. To allow for even cooking, don't overlap the slices; cook in batches if necessary.
4. Cook for 20 minutes, shaking the basket every 5 minutes. After 20 minutes, increase the air fryer temperature to 330°F and cook another 2 minutes, shaking the basket every 30 seconds. Remove the apples from the basket before they get too dark.
5. Spread the chips out onto paper towels to cool completely, at least 5 minutes. Repeat with the remaining apple slices until they're all cooked.

Thick-crust Pepperoni Pizza

Servings: 2   **Cooking Time: 10 Mins.**

Ingredients:

♦ 10 oz. Purchased fresh pizza dough (not a prebaked crust)

♦ Olive oil spray

♦ ¼ C. Purchased pizza sauce

♦ 10 slices Sliced pepperoni

♦ ⅓ C. Purchased shredded Italian 3- or 4-cheese blend

Directions:

1. Preheat the air fryer to 400°F.

2. Generously coat the inside of a 6-inch round cake pan for a small air fryer, a 7-inch round cake pan for a medium air fryer, or an 8-inch round cake pan for a large model with olive oil spray.

3. Set the dough in the pan and press it to fill the bottom in an even, thick layer. Spread the sauce over the dough, then top with the pepperoni and cheese.

4. When the machine is at temperature, set the pan in the basket and air-fry undisturbed for 10 minutes, or until puffed, brown, and bubbling.

5. Use kitchen tongs to transfer the cake pan to a wire rack. Cool for only a minute or so. Use a spatula to loosen the pizza from the pan and lift it out and onto the rack. Continue cooling for a few Mins. before cutting into wedges to serve.

Avocado Fries

Servings: 8 **Cooking Time: 8 Mins.**

Ingredients:

- 2 medium avocados, firm but ripe
- 1 large egg
- ½ tsp. garlic powder
- ¼ tsp. cayenne pepper
- ¼ tsp. salt
- ¾ C. almond flour
- ½ C. finely grated Parmesan cheese
- ½ C. gluten-free breadcrumbs

Directions:

1. Preheat the air fryer to 370°F.
2. Rinse the outside of the avocado with water. Slice the avocado in half, slice it in half again, and then slice it in half once more to get 8 slices. Remove the outer skin. Repeat for the other avocado. Set the avocado slices aside.
3. In a small bowl, whisk the egg, garlic powder, cayenne pepper, and salt in a small bowl. Set aside.
4. In a separate bowl, pour the almond flour.
5. In a third bowl, mix the Parmesan cheese and breadcrumbs.
6. Carefully roll the avocado slices in the almond flour, then dip them in the egg wash, and coat them in the cheese and breadcrumb topping. Repeat until all 16 fries are coated.
7. Liberally spray the air fryer basket with olive oil spray and place the avocado fries into the basket, leaving a little space around the sides between fries. Depending on the size of your air fryer, you may need to cook these in batches.
8. Cook fries for 8 minutes, or until the outer coating turns light brown.
9. Carefully remove, repeat with remaining slices, and then serve warm.

VEGETARIANS RECIPES

Lentil Fritters

Ingredients:

- 1 C. cooked red lentils
- 1 C. riced cauliflower
- ½ medium zucchini, shredded (about 1 cup)
- ¼ C. finely chopped onion
- ¼ tsp. salt
- ¼ tsp. black pepper
- ½ tsp. garlic powder
- ¼ tsp. paprika
- 1 large egg
- ⅓ C. quinoa flour

Directions:

1. Preheat the air fryer to 370°F.
2. In a large bowl, mix the lentils, cauliflower, zucchini, onion, salt, pepper, garlic powder, and paprika. Mix in the egg and flour until a thick dough forms.
3. Using a large spoon, form the dough into 9 large fritters.
4. Liberally spray the air fryer basket with olive oil. Place the fritters into the basket, leaving space around each fritter so you can flip them.
5. Cook for 6 minutes, flip, and cook another 6 minutes.
6. Remove from the air fryer and repeat with the remaining fritters. Serve warm with desired sauce and sides.

Vegetable Couscous

Ingredients:

- 4 oz. white mushrooms, sliced
- ½ medium green bell pepper, julienned
- 1 C. cubed zucchini
- ¼ small onion, slivered
- 1 stalk celery, thinly sliced
- ¼ tsp. ground coriander
- ¼ tsp. ground cumin
- salt and pepper
- 1 tbsp. olive oil
- Couscous
- ¾ C. uncooked couscous
- 1 C. vegetable broth or water
- ½ tsp. salt (omit if using salted broth)

Directions:

1. Combine all vegetables in large bowl. Sprinkle with coriander, cumin, and salt and pepper to taste. Stir well, add olive oil, and stir again to coat vegetables evenly.
2. Place vegetables in air fryer basket and cook at 390°F for 5minutes. Stir and cook for 5 more minutes, until tender.
3. While vegetables are cooking, prepare the couscous: Place broth or water and salt in large saucepan. Heat to boiling, stir in couscous, cover, and remove from heat.
4. Let couscous sit for 5minutes, stir in cooked vegetables, and serve hot.

Mexican Twice Air-fried Sweet Potatoes

Servings: 2   **Cooking Time: 42 Mins.**

Ingredients:

- 2 large sweet potatoes
- olive oil
- salt and freshly ground black pepper
- ⅓ C. diced red onion
- ⅓ C. diced red bell pepper
- ½ C. canned black beans, drained and rinsed
- ½ C. corn kernels, fresh or frozen
- ½ tsp. chili powder
- 1½ C. grated pepper jack cheese, divided
- Jalapeño peppers, sliced

Directions:

1. Preheat the air fryer to 400°F.
2. Rub the outside of the sweet potatoes with olive oil and season with salt and freshly ground black pepper. Transfer the potatoes into the air fryer basket and air-fry at 400°F for 30 minutes, rotating the potatoes a few times during the cooking process.
3. While the potatoes are air-frying, start the potato filling. Preheat a large sauté pan over medium heat on the stovetop. Add the onion and pepper and sauté for a few minutes, until the vegetables start to soften. Add the black beans, corn, and chili powder and sauté for another 3 minutes. Set the mixture aside.
4. Remove the sweet potatoes from the air fryer and let them rest for 5 minutes. Slice off one inch of the flattest side of both potatoes. Scrape the potato flesh out of the potatoes, leaving half an inch of potato flesh around the edge of the potato. Place all the potato flesh into a large bowl and mash it with a fork. Add the black bean mixture and 1 C. of the pepper jack cheese to the mashed sweet potatoes. Season with salt and freshly ground black pepper and mix well. Stuff the hollowed out potato shells with the black bean and sweet potato mixture, mounding the filling high in the potatoes.
5. Transfer the stuffed potatoes back into the air fryer basket and air-fry at 370°F for 10 minutes. Sprinkle the remaining cheese on top of each stuffed potato, lower the heat to 340°F and air-fry for an additional 2 Mins. to melt the cheese. Top with a couple slices of Jalapeño pepper and serve warm with a green salad.

Spinach And Cheese Calzone

Servings: 2   **Cooking Time: 10 Mins.**

Ingredients:

- ⅔ C. frozen chopped spinach, thawed
- 1 C. grated mozzarella cheese
- 1 C. ricotta cheese
- ½ tsp. Italian seasoning
- ½ tsp. salt
- freshly ground black pepper
- 1 store-bought or homemade pizza dough* (about 12 to 16 ounces)
- 2 tbsp. olive oil
- pizza or marinara sauce (optional)

Directions:

1. Drain and squeeze all the water out of the thawed spinach and set it aside. Mix the mozzarella cheese, ricotta cheese, Italian seasoning, salt and freshly ground black pepper together in a bowl. Stir in the chopped spinach.

2. Divide the dough in half. With floured hands or on a floured surface, stretch or roll one half of the dough into a 10-inch circle. Spread half of the cheese and spinach mixture on half of the dough, leaving about one inch of dough empty around the edge.

3. Fold the other half of the dough over the cheese mixture, almost to the edge of the bottom dough to form a half moon. Fold the bottom edge of dough up over the top edge and crimp the dough around the edges in order to make the crust and seal the calzone. Brush the dough with olive oil. Repeat with the second half of dough to make the second calzone.

4. Preheat the air fryer to 360°F.

5. Brush or spray the air fryer basket with olive oil. Air-fry the calzones one at a time for 10 minutes, flipping the calzone over half way through. Serve with warm pizza or marinara sauce if desired.

Pinto Taquitos

Servings: 4   **Cooking Time: 8 Mins.**

Ingredients:

- 12 corn tortillas (6- to 7-inch size)
- Filling
- ½ C. refried pinto beans
- ½ C. grated sharp Cheddar or Pepper Jack cheese
- ¼ C. corn kernels (if frozen, measure after thawing and draining)
- 2 tbsp. chopped green onion
- 2 tbsp. chopped jalapeño pepper (seeds and ribs removed before chopping)
- ½ tsp. lime juice
- ½ tsp. chile powder, plus extra for dusting
- ½ tsp. cumin
- ½ tsp. garlic powder
- oil for misting or cooking spray
- salsa, sour cream, or guacamole for dipping

Directions:

1. Mix together all filling Ingredients.
2. Warm refrigerated tortillas for easier rolling. (Wrap in damp paper towels and microwave for 30 to 60 seconds.)
3. Working with one at a time, place 1 tbsp. of filling on tortilla and roll up. Spray with oil or cooking spray and dust outside with chile powder to taste.
4. Place 6 taquitos in air fryer basket (4 on bottom layer, 2 stacked crosswise on top). Cook at 390°F for 8 minutes, until crispy and brown.
5. Repeat step 4 to cook remaining taquitos.
6. Serve plain or with salsa, sour cream, or guacamole for dipping.

Roasted Vegetable Pita Pizza

Servings: 4   **Cooking Time: 20 Mins.**

Ingredients:

♦ 1 medium red bell pepper, seeded and cut into quarters

♦ 1 tsp. extra-virgin olive oil

♦ ⅛ tsp. black pepper

♦ ⅛ tsp. salt

♦ Two 6-inch whole-grain pita breads

♦ 6 tbsp. pesto sauce

♦ ¼ small red onion, thinly sliced

♦ ½ C. shredded part-skim mozzarella cheese

Directions:

1. Preheat the air fryer to 400°F.

2. In a small bowl, toss the bell peppers with the olive oil, pepper, and salt.

3. Place the bell peppers in the air fryer and cook for 15 minutes, shaking every 5 Mins. to prevent burning.

4. Remove the peppers and set aside. Turn the air fryer temperature down to 350°F.

5. Lay the pita bread on a flat surface. Cover each with half the pesto sauce; then top with even portions of the red bell peppers and onions. Sprinkle cheese over the top. Spray the air fryer basket with olive oil mist.

6. Carefully lift the pita bread into the air fryer basket with a spatula.

7. Cook for 5 to 8 minutes, or until the outer edges begin to brown and the cheese is melted.

8. Serve warm with desired sides.

Veggie Burgers

Servings: 4   **Cooking Time: 15 Mins.**

Ingredients:

- 2 cans black beans, rinsed and drained
- ½ C. cooked quinoa
- ½ C. shredded raw sweet potato
- ¼ C. diced red onion
- 2 tsp. ground cumin
- 1 tsp. coriander powder
- ½ tsp. salt
- oil for misting or cooking spray
- 8 slices bread
- suggested toppings: lettuce, tomato, red onion, Pepper Jack cheese, guacamole

Directions:

1. In a medium bowl, mash the beans with a fork.
2. Add the quinoa, sweet potato, onion, cumin, coriander, and salt and mix well with the fork.
3. Shape into 4 patties, each ¾-inch thick.
4. Mist both sides with oil or cooking spray and also mist the basket.
5. Cook at 390°F for 15minutes.
6. Follow the recipe for Toast, Plain & Simple.
7. Pop the veggie burgers back in the air fryer for a minute or two to reheat if necessary.
8. Serve on the toast with your favorite burger toppings.

Cheese Ravioli

 Servings: 4   **Cooking Time: 9 Mins.**

Ingredients:

- 1 egg
- ¼ C. milk
- 1 C. breadcrumbs
- 2 tsp. Italian seasoning
- ⅛ tsp. ground rosemary
- ¼ tsp. basil
- ¼ tsp. parsley
- 9-ounce package uncooked cheese ravioli
- ¼ C. flour
- oil for misting or cooking spray

Directions:

1. Preheat air fryer to 390°F.
2. In a medium bowl, beat together egg and milk.
3. In a large plastic bag, mix together the breadcrumbs, Italian seasoning, rosemary, basil, and parsley.
4. Place all the ravioli and the flour in a bag or a bowl with a lid and shake to coat.
5. Working with a handful at a time, drop floured ravioli into egg wash. Remove ravioli, letting excess drip off, and place in bag with breadcrumbs.
6. When all ravioli are in the breadcrumbs' bag, shake well to coat all pieces.
7. Dump enough ravioli into air fryer basket to form one layer. Mist with oil or cooking spray. Dump the remaining ravioli on top of the first layer and mist with oil.
8. Cook for 5minutes. Shake well and spray with oil. Break apart any ravioli stuck together and spray any spots you missed the first time.
9. Cook 4 Mins. longer, until ravioli puff up and are crispy golden brown.

Thai Peanut Veggie Burgers

🍜 Servings: 6	🍲 Cooking Time: 14 Mins.

Ingredients:

♦ One 15.5-ounce can cannellini beans

♦ 1 tsp. minced garlic

♦ ¼ C. chopped onion

♦ 1 Thai chili pepper, sliced

♦ 2 tbsp. natural peanut butter

♦ ½ tsp. black pepper

♦ ½ tsp. salt

♦ ⅓ C. all-purpose flour (optional)

♦ ½ C. cooked quinoa

♦ 1 large carrot, grated

♦ 1 C. shredded red cabbage

♦ ¼ C. peanut dressing

♦ ¼ C. chopped cilantro

♦ 6 Hawaiian rolls

♦ 6 butterleaf lettuce leaves

Directions:

1. Preheat the air fryer to 350°F.

2. To a blender or food processor fitted with a metal blade, add the beans, garlic, onion, chili pepper, peanut butter, pepper, and salt. Pulse for 5 to 10 seconds. Do not over process. The mixture should be coarse, not smooth.

3. Remove from the blender or food processor and spoon into a large bowl. Mix in the cooked quinoa and carrots. At this point, the mixture should begin to hold together to form small patties. If the dough appears to be too sticky (meaning you likely processed a little too long), add the flour to hold the patties together.

4. Using a large spoon, form 8 equal patties out of the batter.

5. Liberally spray a metal trivet with olive oil spray and set in the air fryer basket. Place the patties into the basket, leaving enough space to be able to turn them with a spatula.

6. Cook for 7 minutes, flip, and cook another 7 minutes.

7. Remove from the heat and repeat with additional patties.

8. To serve, place the red cabbage in a bowl and toss with peanut dressing and cilantro. Place the veggie burger on a bun, and top with a slice of lettuce and cabbage slaw.

VEGETABLE SIDE DISHES RECIPES

Tandoori Cauliflower

Servings: 4   **Cooking Time: 10 Mins.**

Ingredients:

- ½ C. Plain full-fat yogurt (not Greek yogurt)
- 1½ tsp. Yellow curry powder, purchased or homemade (see the headnote)
- 1½ tsp. Lemon juice
- ¾ tsp. Table salt (optional)
- 4½ C. (about 1 lb. 2 ounces) 2-inch cauliflower florets

Directions:

1. Preheat the air fryer to 400°F.

2. Whisk the yogurt, curry powder, lemon juice, and salt (if using) in a large bowl until uniform. Add the florets and stir gently to coat the florets well and evenly. Even better, use your clean, dry hands to get the yogurt mixture down into all the nooks of the florets.

3. When the machine is at temperature, transfer the florets to the basket, spreading them gently into as close to one layer as you can. Air-fry for 10 minutes, tossing and rearranging the florets twice so that any covered or touching parts are exposed to the air currents, until lightly browned and tender if still a bit crunchy.

4. Pour the contents of the basket onto a wire rack. Cool for at least 5 Mins. before serving, or serve at room temperature.

Fried Cauliflowerwith Parmesan Lemon Dressing

Servings: 2	Cooking Time: 12 Mins.

Ingredients:

- 4 C. cauliflower florets (about half a large head)
- 1 tbsp. olive oil
- salt and freshly ground black pepper
- 1 tsp. finely chopped lemon zest
- 1 tbsp. fresh lemon juice (about half a lemon)
- ¼ C. grated Parmigiano-Reggiano cheese
- 4 tbsp. extra virgin olive oil
- ¼ tsp. salt
- lots of freshly ground black pepper
- 1 tbsp. chopped fresh parsley

Directions:

1. Preheat the air fryer to 400°F.
2. Toss the cauliflower florets with the olive oil, salt and freshly ground black pepper. Air-fry for 12 minutes, shaking the basket a couple of times during the cooking process.
3. While the cauliflower is frying, make the dressing. Combine the lemon zest, lemon juice, Parmigiano-Reggiano cheese and olive oil in a small bowl. Season with salt and lots of freshly ground black pepper. Stir in the parsley.
4. Turn the fried cauliflower out onto a serving platter and drizzle the dressing over the top.

Fried Okra

Servings: 4   **Cooking Time: 8 Mins.**

Ingredients:

♦ 1 lb. okra

♦ 1 large egg

♦ 1 tbsp. milk

♦ 1 tsp. salt, divided

♦ ½ tsp. black pepper, divided

♦ ¼ tsp. paprika

♦ ¼ tsp. thyme

♦ ½ C. cornmeal

♦ ½ C. all-purpose flour

Directions:

1. Preheat the air fryer to 400°F.

2. Cut the okra into ½-inch rounds.

3. In a medium bowl, whisk together the egg, milk, ½ tsp. of the salt, and ¼ tsp. of black pepper. Place the okra into the egg mixture and toss until well coated.

4. In a separate bowl, mix together the remaining ½ tsp. of salt, the remaining ¼ tsp. of black pepper, the paprika, the thyme, the cornmeal, and the flour. Working in small batches, dredge the egg-coated okra in the cornmeal mixture until all the okra has been breaded.

5. Place a single layer of okra in the air fryer basket and spray with cooking spray. Cook for 4 minutes, toss to check for crispness, and cook another 4 minutes. Repeat in batches, as needed.

Simple Roasted Sweet Potatoes

🥣 Servings: 2	🍲 Cooking Time: 45 Mins.

Ingredients:

♦ 2 10- to 12-ounce sweet potato(es)

Directions:

1. Preheat the air fryer to 350°F .

2. Prick the sweet potato(es) in four or five different places with the tines of a flatware fork (not in a line but all around).

3. When the machine is at temperature, set the sweet potato(es) in the basket with as much air space between them as possible. Air-fry undisturbed for 45 minutes, or until soft when pricked with a fork.

4. Use kitchen tongs to transfer the sweet potato(es) to a wire rack. Cool for 5 Mins. before serving.

Green Peas With Mint

Ingredients:

- 1 C. shredded lettuce
- 1 10-ounce package frozen green peas, thawed
- 1 tbsp. fresh mint, shredded
- 1 tsp. melted butter

Directions:

1. Lay the shredded lettuce in the air fryer basket.
2. Toss together the peas, mint, and melted butter and spoon over the lettuce.
3. Cook at 360°F for 5minutes, until peas are warm and lettuce wilts.

Okra

Ingredients:

- 7–8 oz. fresh okra
- 1 egg
- 1 C. milk
- 1 C. breadcrumbs
- ½ tsp. salt
- oil for misting or cooking spray

Directions:

1. Remove stem ends from okra and cut in ½-inch slices.
2. In a medium bowl, beat together egg and milk. Add okra slices and stir to coat.
3. In a sealable plastic bag or container with lid, mix together the breadcrumbs and salt.
4. Remove okra from egg mixture, letting excess drip off, and transfer into bag with breadcrumbs.
5. Shake okra in crumbs to coat well.
6. Place all of the coated okra into the air fryer basket and mist with oil or cooking spray. Okra doesn't need to cook in a single layer, nor is it necessary to spray all sides at this point. A good spritz on top will do.
7. Cook at 390°F for 5minutes. Shake basket to redistribute and give it another spritz as you shake.
8. Cook 5 more minutes. Shake and spray again. Cook for 2 Mins. longer or until golden brown and crispy.

Sesame Carrots And Sugar Snap Peas

🥣 Servings: 4	🍲 Cooking Time: 16 Mins.

Ingredients:

- 1 lb. carrots, peeled sliced on the bias (½-inch slices)
- 1 tsp. olive oil
- salt and freshly ground black pepper
- ⅓ C. honey
- 1 tbsp. sesame oil
- 1 tbsp. soy sauce
- ½ tsp. minced fresh ginger
- 4 oz. sugar snap peas (about 1 cup)
- 1½ tsp. sesame seeds

Directions:

1. Preheat the air fryer to 360°F.

2. Toss the carrots with the olive oil, season with salt and pepper and air-fry for 10 minutes, shaking the basket once or twice during the cooking process.

3. Combine the honey, sesame oil, soy sauce and minced ginger in a large bowl. Add the sugar snap peas and the air-fried carrots to the honey mixture, toss to coat and return everything to the air fryer basket.

4. Turn up the temperature to 400°F and air-fry for an additional 6 minutes, shaking the basket once during the cooking process.

5. Transfer the carrots and sugar snap peas to a serving bowl. Pour the sauce from the bottom of the cooker over the vegetables and sprinkle sesame seeds over top. Serve immediately.

Shoestring Butternut Squash Fries

🍲 Servings: 3	🍲 Cooking Time: 16 Mins.

Ingredients:

♦ 1 lb. 2 oz. Spiralized butternut squash strands

♦ Vegetable oil spray

♦ To taste Coarse sea salt or kosher salt

Directions:

1. Preheat the air fryer to 375°F .

2. Place the spiralized squash in a big bowl. Coat the strands with vegetable oil spray, toss well, coat again, and toss several times to make sure all the strands have been oiled.

3. When the machine is at temperature, pour the strands into the basket and spread them out into as even a layer as possible. Air-fry for 16 minutes, tossing and rearranging the strands every 4 minutes, or until they're lightly browned and crisp.

4. Pour the contents of the basket into a serving bowl, add salt to taste, and toss well before serving hot.

Printed in Great Britain
by Amazon